Extremely Efficient Social Media Strategies for Network Marketing

Become a Pro Network / Multi-Level Marketer by Using Step by Step Digital Marketing Methods for Finding Success with Your MLM Business

By Graham Fisher, Ray Schreiter & Tom Higdon

"Extremely Efficient Social Media Strategies for Network Marketing: Become a Pro Network / Multi-Level Marketer by Using Step by Step Digital Marketing Methods for Finding Success with Your MLM Business" Written by "Neil Sharp", "Ray Schreiter" & "Tom Higdon"

Extremely Efficient Social Media Strategies for Network Marketing is a bundle of the books "Social Media Marketing Mastery", & "Insanely Effective Network and Multi-Level Marketing for Introverts on Social Media". Hope You Enjoy!

Social Media Marketing Mastery

Learn Advanced Digital Marketing Strategies That Will Transform Your Business or Agency on Understanding the Power of Analytics, Facebook Advertising, and Much More

By Graham Fisher

Table of Contents

Introduction

Thank you for downloading *Social Media Marketing Mastery!* This book is going to introduce you to the power of social media marketing, the influence that social media has over your audience and the specific strategies that you need to use to leverage social media for sales conversations today!

As you read through this book, note that there are strategies for every single major social media site out there right now, but you are not required to be on all of these platforms to create the impact that you desire to have. In fact, you can create a massive impact by just existing on two or three platforms and focusing your efforts there. As you will learn about in this book, social media is powerful and the more focused and present you are in getting in front of your audience and putting your message out there, the easier it will be for you to convert on social media.

In addition to using this book to help get you started, you should keep it on hand to walk you through the process of growing your presence, too. Social media has a lot to offer, which means that there is also a lot to learn and embracing that learning curve can be rather challenging. Keeping this book handy as you learn how to use social media and leverage it is a great opportunity for you to ensure that you always have access to the information that you need to succeed on the internet. That way, whether you need support in increasing your engagement or support in creating your next paid advertisement, you have everything you need at the tip of your fingers.

Lastly, note that social media is a powerful giant and once you position your brand in it, there is no way that you will not be able to generate some degree of success online. That being said, your success and the timeline of your success is not guaranteed. I say this not to scare you away or lead you into believing that there is a big chance that you will fail, but to remind you that your success on social media is solely reliant on your willingness to try, embrace the learning curve, understand how this machine works, and put yourself out there. The ones who make it big on social media are the ones who continue trying, educate themselves, stay consistent, and do what they can to stay relevant and interesting to their audience. The more you gauge your audience (which you will learn how to in this very book,) the more you are going to be able to create content that appeals to them, thus enabling you to grow effectively on social media. With that being said, if you are ready to get your business out there and conquer social media, let's begin!

Chapter 1: The Importance of Social Media

Before we dig into the strategies around social media, I want you to get really clear about what potential you are tapping into here. When you understand how social media works, why it is so relevant and vital in modern business, and what it can do for you and your company, understanding how to fit it into your company's marketing strategy becomes a lot easier. You likely already have some information about the value of social media, or you would not be here, reading this book. That being said, you might not know just how valuable social media is and what exactly it has to offer for you and your growing company. In order to give you an insight into this marketing giant that can completely change the future of your company forever, let's take a deeper look into the importance of social media in modern business.

How Social Media Influences Recognition

Perhaps one of the biggest benefits that we gain from social media is that social media influences your brand recognition by making it easier for your target audience to know who you are, remember who you are, and recognize you when they see you. Think of this as building a relationship with your audience: the more your audience sees you on the internet, the more they are going to remember your company, recall what your brand is about and what you have to offer, and if they like you or not. You create recognition every single time you post, engage, or create content to share online. This means that every organic and paid piece of marketing that leaves your company's accounts to begin circulating the internet will be generating brand recognition for you, creating an excellent opportunity for you to begin making more money with your company online.

They say that an individual needs to see a company cross their page at least 13 times before they fully remember who that company is, what they have to offer, and whether or not they are interested in that company. If they are interested, they will likely click through or pay attention a few times in those initial 13 points of contact, after which they will likely begin following your page. The more you are seen, the greater your chances of being discovered by your target audience online. This means that following these points of contact, any time your brand is mentioned, seen offline, or seen elsewhere online, your audience will recognize you and will pay attention to whatever it is that you may be offering.

With that in mind, it makes sense why consistency is so important online: if you are not consistent you will miss out on the opportunity to develop those points of recognition, thus causing you to lose out on the opportunity to generate traction online. You need to make sure that your number one strategy on social media is consistency: consistently posting new updates, consistently engaging with your audience, and consistently creating the opportunity for recognition and growth to occur.

How Social Media Influences Sales

One of the biggest struggles people have on social media is converting recognition and engagement into sales traffic. Fortunately, this is an easy situation to resolve, as long as you are willing to spend some time understanding the cause of your problem. If you are brand new to the internet and have not accumulated enough time online yet to determine whether or not this is a problem for you, it is still valuable for you to understand these strategies so that you can start off strong. The first thing you need to do when it comes to using social media to influence sales is to make sure that you are targeting the right audience. You will learn how to do this for each platform later on, but targeting the right audience is important to ensure that you are accumulating an audience of people who are more likely to convert into paying customers. If you are not clear enough in your targeting, you may find yourself accumulating an audience of people who are not actually interested in your company or in purchasing from you, which can result in you having difficulty gaining conversions online.

The second strategy to begin converting your followers is to make sure that every single post you make in regards to sales is clear, relevant, and interesting. You want to keep all of your posts designed in a way that is actually going to entice your audience to pay attention so that they have a reason to read them and follow through on the call to action. Remember: your audience is seeing a lot of sales posts every single day, so you need to be consistent and continue sharing relevant sales that are going to actually encourage your audience to pay attention and follow through on purchasing from your company. As you continue to build recognition and credibility with your audience, your audience will begin considering you over anyone else marketing online because they see you as being consistent and relevant in the online space.

Finally, you need to make sure that your sales are actually relevant to your audience. You do not want to be selling to an audience that does not care about what you have to offer. If your sales are not picking up or if you are not gaining any traction at all, make sure that you take some time to research your target audience and position your sales and products accordingly. Sometimes, one small thing can be completely off which leads to your audience no longer paying attention or feeling disinterested in something that would otherwise be great for them. Taking the time to really get to know your audience by learning more about what they are looking for and how they want to both find it and experience it will ensure that everything you share with your audience is relevant to what they are looking for.

How Social Media Benefits Your Business Directly

Social media will benefit your business in many direct ways, with the most important way likely being the increase in sales that come from your target audience. That being said, your social media presence will actually have many additional benefits to your company beyond being able to increase your sales numbers. In addition to creating brand recognition, driving greater sales, and supporting you in tapping into a global audience, social media will actually reduce your costs. When you are on social media, the cost of doing business is reduced because you can take advantage of organic and low-investment paid advertising options, which are both significantly cheaper than standard advertising practices. In fact, most businesses exist exclusively online nowadays because the cost of doing business online is so much cheaper than doing business in person. For businesses that cannot operate exclusively online, they are using the internet as much as possible to minimize their costs of doing business, thus increasing their profit margin. With thanks to the increasing number of clients and decreasing costs of doing business, most brands are seeing significant increases in their ability to run successful brands largely in thanks to social media.

In addition to being more cost-effective, social media also makes marketing more time effective, too. When you advertise on social media, the majority of your marketing becomes significantly easier because you can do it yourself rather than having to have other people do it for you. In the past, even a simple newspaper advertisement required you to connect with the advertisement director of the newspaper and a design agency who could design your newspaper ad. Although this is only two additional people, it can take a significant amount of time to get your materials in front of an audience. Furthermore, the audience is not targeted, so you are spending a lot of money to get seen by people who are not directly a part of your target audience, thus meaning that you are paying a lot to get seen by many irrelevant people. On social media, you can easily create a piece of content, target it, and have it seen by tens, hundreds, thousands, and even hundreds of thousands of people in your target audience. Social media has a massive power to reduce the amount of time that it takes to get your advertisements out there, meaning that you can increase the volume of your advertising and have every single advertisement making a much larger impact than any print advertisement likely could. This means that advertising has not only gotten cheaper, but it has also gotten far more effective.

The ROI of Social Media Marketing

When it comes to social media marketing, many companies find that 100% of their audience finds them on social media and purchases through them as a result of having found them on social media. This is especially true for companies where their entire business is run online, as social media provides a much larger opportunity to connect with your audience quickly and from anywhere in the world. That being said, even brick and mortar companies are having a greater influx of business from their social media strategies, as social media allows people to discover businesses that are in their own local vicinity. Businesses that target tourists are also having an easier time getting their name out there on a global level, allowing them to increase their global traffic all through social media.

The biggest reason why it is so important for even brick and mortar businesses to be online is that these days, most individuals are going to search for a company on Google or on a social media giant to see if they exist online. If they do not know of an actual company, they will search for that company's niche online and find whoever comes up to satisfy their search query. If you do not come up, that individual will not have the opportunity to learn about and do business with you, thus creating a missed connection. If, however, you do come up and you have invested time in building a positive reputation online then when your potential audience member finds you online, they will be able to both discover that you exist *and* see that you have a lot of social proof validating that you are a positive company. As a result, they are more likely to choose you over anyone else because they can see that you are good at what you do.

These days, it is not enough to use passive marketing strategies as a way to get in front of your audience. Leaving your name around on flyers, passing out your business cards, and putting your company in the newspaper may be effective for some businesses, but virtually every business is going to benefit even more from getting on social media and building a presence. Your recognition and social proof alone will massively increase your conversions, thus allowing your business to grow rapidly and consistently in the new age of digital marketing.

Chapter 2: The Social Media Impact

Social media clearly has a massive impact, but you may be wondering just how far that impact reaches and the specifics around how the impact works. These days, the social media impact works in four very specific and modern ways: through influencers, videos, virtual and augmented reality, and specific targeting. When you take advantage of these four strategies, you maximize your impact which results in you being seen by a significant number of people in your target audience. The more you continue to share and leverage these four strategies, the further your reach will gain, and the more significant your social media impact will become. It is extremely powerful to have your social media efforts tapping into these four areas, which is why we are going to explore them and how they work, now. Note that each will work slightly differently across each platform, so you will need to pay attention to the important steps for implementing these strategies on the platforms that you will be targeting with your business.

Mainstream Influencer Potential

One of the most powerful strategies for leveraging social media marketing in the modern world is tapping into the mainstream influencer potential. For decades, social marketing has been a powerful leverage for any company that is looking to broaden their audience. Relying on word of mouth has existed since business first became a "thing," as word of mouth was the only marketing opportunity people had at that time. Despite the face of marketing having gone through many changes over the years, the very foundation of marketing remains the same as people are still more likely to trust in companies whom they have received a personalized recommendation for. In the modern world, we have social media which means that it is easier than ever for large networks of people to rapidly learn about companies that they will love and begin doing business with those companies. As a result, a unique niche industry has popped up where individuals specialize in building large networks and marketing products to these networks. These individuals are known as influencers, and they are largely responsible for the circulation of products when it comes to generating a massive buzz through word of mouth in relatively minimal timing.

Influencers are masters at word of mouth marketing, and when they are leveraged effectively, they can help put your brand in front of tens of thousands or even hundreds of thousands of new individuals in a rapid period of time. For a newer brand that is looking to expand or an older brand who is looking to grow, having the support of influencers is a powerful way to get out there quickly and take massive strides toward your sales goals. The key in getting in front of the masses and creating these quick shifts in your marketing success through influencers is to make sure that the products or services you are offering are relevant to the influencers that you are approaching. After all, they specialize in catering to a very specific audience so that their audience is active and ready to purchase the products that they market toward them. They spend a lot of time building up their niche audiences and developing trust with these audiences so that they can connect the brands who share the same target audience and their customers together through their own trial and errors with new products. That being said, trust is a large factor between an influencer and their audience, as their audience trust them only to recommend products that are actually high quality and that will actually fulfill a need or desire in their audiences' lives. If your products are low quality or highly irrelevant, you may find it hard to get in front of a real influencer and have them agree to work with you because they do not want to lose their credibility with their audience.

Beyond having these key factors in place to ensure that you are approaching influencers who will actually want to work with you, it is also important that you are approaching mainstream influencers. Many brands make the mistake of working together with individuals who are not truly influencers: such as those who only have hundreds or even a few thousand followers. If you really want to make an impact, you need to get beyond these small influencers and get into the real mainstream influencers who are exceptional at what they do. It is important that you validate every influencer that you seek to work with before you actually invite them to do a deal with you or approach them to consider working with you because you do not want to be wasting your time with smaller influencers. Remember, your time and products are worth money and you need to be thinking like a big-time business owner and only investing in the things that are going to bring you back a significant return on your investment. If you agree to open an affiliate deal with someone who is not even truly an affiliate and you send them free product only to have one or two sales made out of that exchange, you are not getting enough of a return back on your investment. At this rate, you will be losing far more money than you could be making with a better marketing plan, so you need to avoid doing this. Always validate your influencers by making sure that they have the right audience, the right pull with their audience, and the means to work toward getting you the best return on your investment possible. If you cannot validate that an influencer will be able to do this for you, it may not be in your best interest to work with one.

Video Advertisements

Video content has steadily increased in popularity over the past few years, first with the rise of YouTube stars and then with the introduction of Vine, a company which officially shut down their platform in January of 2017. Video content has been created for a myriad of reasons, from offering entertainment or showing off ones' skills to providing education or knowledge. Each person or brand has its own unique way to use video content as an opportunity to generate more traction with their audience and increase the amount of value that they have to offer people. The more you tap into using video to create content for your fans, including through advertisements, the more you are going to be able to connect with your audience in a way that they actually prefer connecting through.

To give you an idea of how powerful video content is: video content on the internet is expected to surpass the number of accumulated cable watch minutes in 2019. In other words, people are watching more video on the internet than they are watching cable TV these days, which says a lot since it was not too long ago that soap operas and reality TV were taking the world by storm! Getting in on this video advertising wave is crucial if you want to meet your audience where they are at, effectively connect with them, and begin making massive conversion ratios to help you increase your sales numbers through social media.

There are many reasons why video content is so powerful, but the biggest reason is that your video content is going to enable you to begin making a more personable connection with your followers from all around the world. When you connect with your following through video content, they get to see your face or the faces behind your brand which allows them to feel like they are right there with you, having a conversation and getting to know you. Furthermore, they get to have the opportunity to get to know your products or your services in a visual manner, which allows them to actually *see* what you have to offer. This visual connection makes the experience far more interactive, which increases your audience's likelihood of purchasing from you because now they can actually see what you have to offer and they get to have the opportunity to fall in love with it through visual connection. If you have a product to offer, you can create a sense of desire in your audience by showing them how it works and giving them a physical demonstration of what they can do with the product and how it will change or enhance their life. If you have a service to offer, you can begin offering free pieces of content or offerings with your audience to give them an idea of what it is like to work with you, thus enabling them to see whether or not they resonate with you. For example, if you are a business coach you could offer a free twenty-minute training on how to research for hashtags in your business or how to optimize your Facebook page to get more viewers. As a result of giving away this content for free, you show your audience what it feels like to work with you which makes them interested in learning more from you or seeing what else you have to offer.

Video content can be shared in many ways these days, ranging from sharing video content in your story feeds on Facebook or Instagram to sharing live video feeds on almost any of the major networking sites. You can also upload video content to video hosting platforms like YouTube or Vimeo and share content from there across all of your other platforms. However, you choose to share your video content, make sure that you are sharing in a way that provides value to your audience, generates a "face" for your company that your audience can connect to, and encourages your audience to purchase a product or service from you.

Virtual and Augmented Reality Filters

As video content continues to grow, more people are not only consuming video content but are also creating and sharing it themselves to be seen by their friends and their own followers. As a brand, this gives you a unique opportunity to get in front of your audience by creating filters that your audience can use when they are sharing content with their followers. Virtual and augmented reality filters are a great opportunity to put your brand in front of your audience and begin building word of mouth marketing connections through video content.

A great example of brands who are already using this feature are Kylie Cosmetics and Gucci Beauty which are both using Instagram filters to share their products with their audience. When you use these filters, you are able to see their beauty lines show up on your screen and you can interact with them in a way that lets you enjoy sharing video or pictures with your audience. Then, your audience sees them, and they share with the same filter and, before you know it, your brand is spreading a lot further all through a virtual or augmented reality filter. As more people see the products or services being shown in your filter, people begin to notice that they are interested in learning more, so they search out your company and begin exploring what you have to offer. As a result, they may purchase products or services from your company, or they may begin following you and getting to know your brand so that they can purchase in the future.

Creating these filters may seem challenging, but most platforms with story sharing features have created the opportunity to create your filters directly in the app. That, or you can work together with a designer to have the filter created specifically for your brand. Of course, these filters do come with a price tag attached to them, but if you are willing to pay that price, which often starts around $15/day, you can easily begin promoting a filter that shares your brand with your audience in a bigger way.

Specific Targeting Opportunities

All social media platforms are now catering to the fact that there is a natural and welcomed exchange happening on their platforms. Brands are arriving to share their products, and customers are arriving to purchase them. As a result, platforms are narrowing in on the opportunity to help connect brands and customers, and they make a percentage of profit off of this connection. Of course, you can use opportunities like organic marketing which will cost you nothing and earn you a following and sales, but you can also use more effective strategies like paid marketing which will cost money but will get you a larger audience to market to. Because they are able to provide this leverage, social media companies are also regularly creating new opportunities for you to actually target your audience and get directly in front of the people who are most likely to purchase from you.

Back in the day, people would pay good money for advertisements that would be seen by a massive number of people: many of which had nothing to do with their audience and would never become a part of their audience. Still, because they were getting seen by so many people, they would pay a lot of money for placement. These days, you can pay significantly less money and get seen by the same number of people from your target audience as you did in the past, but without having to get seen by non-targeted audience members. Because you are not getting seen by as many people overall, you do not have to pay as much as the ad placement elsewhere will simply be purchased by people who are more likely to resonate with that audience or the audience that is not yours. By that knowledge, if you were to pay the same amount in advertising fees as people were paying just a decade ago, you would get seen by a massive portion of your target audience, and you would have a huge opportunity to convert higher and faster through that same investment.

There are ways that you can organically target your audience: such as by posting relevant content with relevant keywords and hashtags to get in front of them, and there are ways that you can pay to target your audience, such as through paid advertisements or boosted posts. Both of these are a great opportunity to be getting in front of your audience, so it is important that every single thing you share online engages in targeting your audience in one way or another through these strategies.

Chapter 3: Positioning Yourself Online

Knowing where to spend your time online can be tricky, especially when there are so many platforms out there. From Facebook to LinkedIn, there are several social media "giants" that have multiple millions of active monthly users, thus allowing you to get in front of a large segment of your audience just by using one platform. That being said, you do want to make sure that you hedge yourself from risk by spreading yourself out across a few platforms to make sure that you are always getting seen and growing. Typically, investing your time in growing on 2-3 platforms is the best approach to ensure that you are getting seen by your audience and that if anything changes on one of the platforms that results in you not getting seen as much you still have other platforms to rely on. For example, if algorithms shift and you stop getting seen as often or if one of them were to go down for a period of time, you would still be seen on other platforms.

In this chapter, we are going to explore how you can get seen online by choosing the right platforms for your business. You will discover which platform hosts your target audience, which ones will give you the best opportunity to share your unique business with your audience, and the basics of how they can be used. By the end of this chapter, you will be able to choose which platforms you should be on so that you can achieve your social media goals with your business.

Who is Facebook for?

Facebook is the most versatile platform that virtually every business needs to be on in one way or another. Facebook has the broadest audience with people from all age groups spending time on the platform on a regular basis. This platform also offers you a broad range of ways to connect with your audience so that you can create several avenues of interaction with your audience, allowing you to have the best opportunity to stimulate engagement with your potential clients. Beyond how diverse the age and gender range are on Facebook, it is also the largest social media platform on the internet to date. Facebook has more than 1.32 billion daily active users, which makes it 40% more popular than any other platform out there as of 2018.

Facebook is a great storytelling platform that allows you to combine the features of video, photograph, written content, and link sharing so that you can begin creating a story brand for your audience. You can use the platform to share live video feeds of your company and/or your products and services, to share images of your new products or sales, to write stories or posts about what your company has been up to lately, and to share links from other social sites or from your website or blog. Because of how versatile this platform is for sharing content on, it is ideal for virtually everyone to get on it with their brand and start sharing something. Even if you are not going to be sharing a lot of content on Facebook, at least generating a small presence is helpful in getting seen and found by your audience.

Who is Instagram for?

Instagram is another great visual storytelling platform that is similar to Facebook but slightly different in nature. Where Facebook has a more versatile feed for what you can share and how Instagram relies solely on sharing square pictures or videos with your audience, in addition to sharing your pictures or videos on your wall, you can also share stories, live feeds, 1-10-minute videos on your IGTV channel, and direct messages or videos. Instagram is a powerful platform for brands who have products or services that can be showcased through photographs. In many cases, most brands can in one way or another have a photographic element to their brand, making Instagram a powerful resource for many brands from many different industries.

When it comes to deciding whether or not Instagram is right for you, the biggest thing to consider is its target audience. Instagram tends to have a younger audience than other platforms, with its most popular age range being 18-34-year-old people. It seems to have a fairly balanced gender spread, meaning that regardless of what gender you target with your brand you can still find a way to incorporate Instagram into your social media marketing strategy as long as you share the same targeted age range.

Instagram is another powerful social media giant, as Facebook owns it. This means that if you want to use two platforms that are intricately integrated and that can grow together almost seamlessly, Instagram and Facebook are great choices. You can use Instagram to create posts for both Instagram and Facebook by simply sharing your Instagram posts to the Facebook platform. You can also use Facebook to create paid marketing campaigns for your Instagram account. They both work together to support you in having a powerful marketing strategy online so, as long as your age group meets that which is already on Instagram, combining these two can be highly effective.

Who is Google for?

Google has provided a wonderful opportunity to connect with your audience by giving you the opportunity to develop a presence on this massive search engine and use its Google Hangouts feature as an opportunity to connect with others. Although it is significantly less popular than other platforms, Google Hangouts is still a good place to spend time online if you want to have a platform for direct peer to peer conversations between you and your audience. Many businesses use Google Hangouts to facilitate group chats, video calls, or voice calls between themselves and their audience as it enables a more personalized approach.

The biggest benefit of using Google Hangouts to communicate with your audience is that it gives you the same features as your phone would between text, video, and calling, but it is not going to charge you international calling fees or anything of the sorts. In a sense, you can use Google Hangouts to enable your customers to have phone access to you from all around the world.

Who is Twitter for?

Twitter is a powerful platform for businesses who want to get in on the conversation and stay relevant with their audience. More than 326 million users visit Twitter on a monthly basis to get involved in the conversation, stay connected with their audiences, and market their businesses. Twitter is largely mobile-based platform with more than 80% of its users accessing the platform from their mobile devices and connecting with each other through the mobile application. As a result, Twitter itself targets mobile users, and any brand who wants to get on Twitter and build a presence should do the same by ensuring that their entire online platform, including their website, is mobile friendly.

The gender spread on Twitter is fairly balanced, with about 48% of users being female and 52% of users being male. The most popular age range for Twitter is 30-49 years old, as this age range makes up more than a quarter of all of the users on Twitter. Another great thing about Twitter is that the average click-through ratio for people who land on your profile and then head to the link on your page is around 80%. This means that a high number of people who land on your profile upon finding you on Twitter are going to visit your website and spend time researching who you are and what you are about.

Who is YouTube for?

YouTube is different from other platforms as it primarily caters to creating and sharing video content with your audience. In recent years, YouTube has expanded to create more interactive channels, to include direct messaging, and to offer live video features so that you can share real-time with your audience just like you can on Facebook or Instagram. Even so, YouTube continues to be primarily a video-based search engine where contributors can generate video content for their audiences and be seen and engaged with through their video sharing.

Because of Instagram and Facebook increasing their own video-based content with features like IGTV on Instagram and the Watch tab on Facebook, as well as both platforms having live video options as well, YouTube has more competition than ever before. However, YouTube continues to generate massive value for users who regularly upload content as the platform has more than 30 million daily users who enjoy watching more than 5 billion videos per day. These videos are created by the more than 50 million content creators who have shared content onto the platform to be viewed by their audience.

YouTube's demographic is 60% male and has more than 80% of users existing outside of the United States. Only 9% of all small business owners are leveraging YouTube as a platform to get in front of their audience, which is shocking considering that YouTube can be used to generate video content which is increasing in popularity. It can also be used to create content and then share that content across other platforms, making YouTube a versatile addition to your social media marketing approach.

Who is LinkedIn for?

LinkedIn is the number one B2B platform on the internet to date. This platform enables professionals to mingle amongst each other and connect with other professionals and companies so that they can advance their own careers and build their brands in this highly professional and interactive network. LinkedIn hosts more than 590 million users with more than 260 million actively visiting the platform every single month. More than 61 million LinkedIn users are considered senior influencers in their industries and more than 40 million of those individuals are known as being key decision makers in their companies.

LinkedIn offers a fairly even playing field for professionals with 56% of users being listed as male and 44% of users being listed as female. 87% of the population on LinkedIn is older than the millennial generation, making this a great platform for anyone looking to connect with professionals who are over the age of 35 years old. LinkedIn has one of the most niched audiences on any social media platform at this time, as it primarily caters to businesses and professionals, which makes it a powerful platform for anyone who really wants to get seen as a part of and grow within the professional industry. For anyone who has a more personalized lifestyle brand that does not cater to or collaborate with professionals, LinkedIn is probably not the right platform to be on.

Chapter 4: Why Use Facebook?

When it comes to developing an online presence, Facebook is one of the most powerful tools that you can possibly use to get your business out there. In the digital age, everyone goes to Facebook to learn about new businesses or to discover more about a business that they have recently learned about. Most individuals will assume that if you are not on Facebook, you are not doing much to get your brand out there since Facebook is one of the most basic platforms to get your business on when it comes to joining the social media world.

That being said, Facebook is not a platform that requires you to be active all the time if you feel that you would have an easier time reaching your demographic elsewhere. Simply having a Facebook page that is updated a few times per week is plenty to ensure that you are visible on Facebook and that should anyone look you up on this platform, they can find you. That way, people know that you exist and that you are relevant and that you are available to be engaged with online.

If you do choose to have a presence on Facebook but not a dominant one, you can also link to your other platforms on Facebook so that people can locate you where you spend your time the most. This is a great way to build a social media funnel so that those who desire to follow you can find you and follow you where you are most active online.

Organic Facebook Marketing

Organic Facebook marketing as a simple and cost-effective strategy for getting your brand in front of your target audience. Organic Facebook marketing refers to all forms of engagement on Facebook that do not cost you or your brand any money. Some examples of organic Facebook marketing include sharing live videos, sharing stories, sharing photographs, and sharing status updates. Facebook is one of the most diverse platforms that you can share on as it provides you with many different opportunities to connect with your audience. The benefit of using Facebook for organic marketing is that you can create many different styles of content thus allowing you to appeal to a broader range of your market.

The biggest advantage of organic Facebook marketing is that it is a free opportunity to get in front of your audience and begin building your brand name. Most Facebook marketing strategies will comprise of a heavily organic basis that also features paid marketing strategies. What I mean by this is that most people will post several pieces of content for free, and then occasional he will promote certain content in order to reach a broader spectrum of their audience. By being selective about the content that you actually choose to pay for it, you can ensure that you are taking full advantage of Facebook as a marketing platform without costing you too much money.

The disadvantage of organic Facebook marketing is that when you do not pay for content to be promoted less of your audience will see the content. Due to Facebook algorithms, when you pay to promote content, you are more likely to get seen both by your existing audience and buy your new audience. This means that having a healthy mixture of both organic and paid promotions on Facebook is your best opportunity to get seen by your target audience so that you can begin converting clients on Facebook.

Building and Optimizing Your Facebook Page

Although you can use a personal Facebook profile to promote your business, your best opportunity to connect with your target audience is through a business page. Facebook has the option for you to create a business page for your brand which allows you to establish your brand as a separate entity, paid to boost posts or create promotions, and help your brand stand apart from other businesses on Facebook. There are many different types of Facebook business pages from ones that are designed specifically to share a video content to ones that are designed to help promote products and make sales, and even others that are simply designed to create a platform for your brand to be discovered.

Creating a business page on Facebook is simple. The first step to begin building your Facebook business page is to go to the desktop version of Facebook, locate the action menu on the left side of the screen, and tap "create a page." From there you will be guided through the process of naming your page [which should be your brand name], choosing the profile picture for your page, and deciding on a cover picture for your page. Once you have designed the basic set up for your page, you can locate your page on Facebook, and begin to update your page with an *about* section, a services section, and any other sections you desire to have on your Facebook page. You can find an entire list of sections available for you to create on your Facebook page by locating the settings menu on your Facebook page and tapping "tabs."

In addition to adjusting these various sections on your page, you should also ensure that you go to the "edit page info" section of your settings so that you can update important information about your business such as a basic description, the category your business falls under, and any contact information that your clients may be able to use to locate you. When you update these sections on your Facebook page, you will ensure that your page is easy to locate and that it provides your clients with important information about your business.

As long as these sections on your Facebook page are filled out, you can ensure that your Facebook page is functional and optimized for any potential clients to locate you. This way, even if you are not relying on Facebook as a primary platform online, you can still rely on your Facebook page to drive traffic to your business. Remember, even if you do not choose to use Facebook as a primary platform for your social media strategies, Facebook does provide you with a solid foundation. Virtually every person who is on the Internet has a Facebook account; this means that a vast majority of people who are looking for your business will first look on Facebook. Having a basic Facebook presence, even without using it frequently, will ensure that there is enough information available for your target audience to find you online.

Posting on Your Facebook Page

As you now know, there are many different styles of content that you can upload on Facebook. Of these contents, styles include things like pictures, videos, status updates, and live video feeds so that your audience can consume a variety of different styles of content. Most brands will use one or two different styles of content as their primary ways of sharing with their audience to ensure that their audience knows what to expect. In addition to making their profile uniform, it also ensures that they only need to master one or two different styles of content to create as opposed to trying to create multiple ones. Larger brands may use a larger variety of content, but this is not necessary for small businesses who are just seeking to master social media.

If you are new to Facebook, you may not know which kind of content is the best for you to start with. Starting with video content is typically the best solution for all brands as video content is currently the most popular style of sharing. In addition to using video content, you can also use photographs, particularly those which have quotes on them, or are accompanied by inspiring quotes and the caption as many audience members in various industries tend to respond positively to this type of content.

Another popular style of sharing that many brands use is sharing blog posts, articles, and other relevant links with their audience in a status update. Ideally, you should be sharing the link to that link back to your website however you can also share trending content from other websites. The key value of linking back to your website when sharing links on Facebook is that you are driving traffic directly to your website. This is excellent for website SEO; it also results in more people landing on your page that is increasing their chances of looking at your services or products.

When you share content on your Facebook business page, it is important that everything you share is relevant to your target audience. If you begin to share content that is irrelevant or low-quality, people will stop following you for fear of having their newsfeed filled with irrelevant or low-quality content. You can prevent this from happening by ensuring that all content you post on your own website is high-quality and that all content you link to is also high-quality. In addition to checking for quality, you can also consider how each piece of content directly serves your audience. If the content does not clearly serve your audience, you should refrain from sharing it all together.

The more consistently you share high-quality and relevant content to your Facebook page, the more people will follow you and continue to pay attention to your posts. Even if you are only sharing a few times per week, this can have a positive impact on your social media presence altogether.

Live Videos

Many brands are leveraging live videos as an opportunity to get in front of their audience in a personal manner. Live videos allow you to live stream what you are currently doing so that you can share with your audience in real time. There are many different ways that live videos can be leveraged to allow you to connect with your audience and create more personalized content., A great example of how some brands are using live videos would include people who use live videos as an opportunity to demo their new products in front of their audience. Another way that people will commonly use live video is to share a demonstration of their services or to help their audience get to know them or their brand on a more personal level. Many brands will do live question and answering sessions or other similar live video formats which enable their audience to get to know them better. Another great benefit to using live video in this way is that you gain the opportunity to identify exactly what your audience cares about, what they are looking for, and how you may be able to serve them better. It is not uncommon for brands to use live video as an opportunity to directly ask their audience questions about their existing products and services so that they can gain a better understanding of what their audience would like to see more of.

Live videos are one of the most powerful tools that you can use on Facebook. Therefore it is important that you incorporate live videos into your Facebook. Even if you are only doing a few live videos per month, using these live streams on a consistent basis enables you to build up a library of video content that is already available, thus allowing your target audience to "binge watch" your video content. When it comes to social media marketing, this can be extremely powerful, thus making it well worth your investment.

If you are not yet clear on how you can leverage live videos for your brand, a great opportunity to learn more is to explore existing brands and see how they are using live video to interact with their audience. Because so many brands are using live videos as an opportunity to connect with their audience, learning about new and interesting ways to connect with your audience through live video can help you stand apart from the crowd. The more creative you are, the better, this means that it is completely safe to try out new strategies. If for any reason your strategy does not work, you can always switch to a new strategy and simply delete the videos that did not work to your desires.

Many people find that they do not feel brave enough to get on a live video stream and begin sharing with their audience. This is a common fear, particularly with those who are not used to being on video. A great way to overcome this fear is to begin going live with your settings set to private on your personal page and practicing speaking in front of the camera. Another great strategy that you can use to begin developing your confidence on camera is to film yourself with the camera on your phone, not the camera on Facebook, and get used to seeing yourself on the screen. For many people, this is a great opportunity to develop confidence in camera so that when they go live, it is easier for them to stay focused and develop great live content.

Facebook Stories

Like live videos, Facebook stories are an excellent platform that you can use to share live behind the scenes content with your audience., Facebook stories leverage 30 seconds or shorter video clips or photographs that allow you to showcase your brand in a different light. The reason why the stories are so effective is that it would be on your actual Facebook timeline, thus allowing you to create a more personalized and unique experience. Many brands will use Facebook stories as an opportunity to create an exclusive relationship with their followers who choose to follow their stories. For example, many brands will use stories as an opportunity to showcase new products or services before they ever announce them officially online, or they will use them as an opportunity to show what it looks like to work for the brand.

Stories on Facebook disappear after 24 hours, thus making them particularly exclusive. Anyone who does not see them when they are live will not ever see them as they will disappear in 24 hours. For this reason, many brands use this as an opportunity to create a special relationship with their audience.

Because Facebook stories disappear within 24 hours, it is important that you share on a consistent basis. The more frequently you use Facebook stories, the more consistently people will check in to see what is going on with your brand. Facebook and Instagram stories do integrate, so if you enjoy using both platforms and you desire to keep both of your story feeds active, you can upload stories to your Instagram business page and share them to your Facebook page. This way, all of the stories that you share on Instagram will also be shared on Facebook thus enabling you to have a broader reach with less time and effort.

Facebook Groups

Facebook groups help you develop an exclusive community on Facebook that can be hosted by your Facebook business page. Many brands are using Facebook groups as an opportunity to develop a community for their followers to stay connected with their brand well also staying connected with each other. A great benefit of using Facebook groups as an opportunity to develop a Social Media community is that a large majority of the content that will go into your Facebook group will be user-generated content, which allows you to create a higher amount of content around your brand without having to actually create it yourself. When you are able to create a community amongst your followers, your brand becomes a lot stronger, and you become more well known. People who enjoy being a part of the community will share your community with others, allowing you to have a lot of free marketing content on Facebook.

When you create a Facebook group, it is important that you create the group with a very clear focus. Many brands will create the group with a focus that only alliance with one aspect of the brand. For example, a makeup artist may use Facebook groups as an opportunity to share tutorials whereas they use other platforms to share tutorials, reviews on products, and other similar makeup related content. By having a clear benefit to being in your Facebook group, you can ensure that people feel motivated to join, engage, and provide their own value and content into your group which will allow growth in your community and greater reach on Facebook.

You create a Facebook group similar to how you create a business page. However, if you want to create a Facebook group that connects with your Facebook business page, you will want to create the group from your business page so that your business page is recognized as the host of the group. This creates a complete integration between your page and your group allowing you to have a broader reach, and greater marketing power on Facebook. You can create a Facebook group from your Facebook page by going to your page finding the tabs section on your page, and locating the tab that says, groups. When you click groups, you will see the option to create your own group related to your Facebook page. When you click that option, you will be walked through the process of creating a group by creating a name, creating a category, and creating a profile picture to be used in the group. You will also be given the opportunity to add people to your group. It is important that you do not add people without permission, as many people do not appreciate this style of marketing and may develop a bad taste for your business. It is better to market your Facebook group on your Facebook page, or personally invite people by talking to them in messenger, as this is a more polite way of inviting people into your group. When you market in this way, your group is more likely to grow faster and then you were able to create a larger community and faster reach through your Facebook group.

Paid Facebook Advertising

Facebook is one of the most popular apps to use for advertising on social media. Through Facebook advertising, you cannot only advertise on Facebook but also on Instagram. There are a variety of paid advertisement features that you can use on Facebook including sponsored posts, boosted posts, and Instagram posts. Advertising on Facebook enables you to get in front of a broad range of people since so many people spend so much time on Facebook. When you are using the Facebook ads platform, you need to ensure that you are using it correctly to avoid spending money on advertisements that do not develop the type of traction that you desire. Because so many people spend their time on Facebook, it is important to ensure that you are targeting your audience correctly. Many small brands will not effectively target their audience which results in them wasting money on Facebook advertisements. Remember, if you are not talking to someone specifically, chances are you are not talking to anyone at all.

The biggest benefit of using paid advertisements on Facebook is that you increase your reach. When you use paid promotions on Facebook, Facebook will target either your existing audience, your existing audience plus their friends, or people who are not already following your page. This gives you an excellent opportunity to choose which audience you desired at target, thus enabling you to reach a larger segment of your audience. Unlike organic marketing on Facebook, using paid promotions enables you to ensure that each post is going to gain maximum traction and get your brand in front of your audience. Because Facebook advertisements are guaranteed to develop some kind of viewership, this does make them highly valuable.

The key disadvantage of using Facebook paid promotional features is that if you do not target your audience correctly, you may end up wasting your money. It is not uncommon for small businesses to fail to target their advertisements effectively, which results in them not getting seen by the right people. If this happens, chances are you will not be seen by people who would be interested in purchasing anything from your business. As a result, if your advertisements are not turning traction, they are considered a waste of money. After all, you do not want your audience filled with people who are unwilling to actually purchased from your company as this is completely pointless.

Creating a Facebook Advertisement

Creating advertisements on Facebook is simple, you will start by creating your Facebook ad account, and then you will simply follow the step-by-step process shown to you on the screen. You can easily open up ads manager account on Facebook by heading to Facebook on your desktop, locating the actions menu on the left side of your screen and then locating the tab that says "ads manager." There you will discover how you can begin creating advertisements on Facebook. There will have the opportunity to decide how you are going to pay for your advertisements, and what page you want to link your ads manager account to.

Once you have opened up your Facebook ad manager account, you are ready to begin creating ads. You will build the advertisements by choosing an objective, creating your target audience, and designing the visual elements of your advertisement. Once you have created the advertisement, all you will need to do is confirm your advertisement and Facebook will begin to promote it. If you choose to do a boosted post the strategy is slightly different, so we will discuss how this unique strategy works at the end of this chapter.

Choosing Your Objective

The first step to creating your Facebook advertisement is deciding what you want the objective of your post to be. There are many different types of objectives that you can choose for your Facebook advertisement. In fact, there are 11 different objectives that you can choose from, ranging from reaching new audience members to converting your audience or even generating sales through your Facebook catalog. You need to pack the advertisement objective that best suits your brands needs based on what you are attempting to achieve through your advertisements. If you are not entirely sure as to what your objective should be, you can always consider using split testing by creating two or three different advertisements with different objectives, allowing you to understand which conversions will work the best. Split advertising is a common paid advertising option that enables brands to better understand what their audience is looking for, what they respond best to you, and how they can best invest their money and paid advertisements in order to get the best return.

Creating Your Ad "Behind the Scenes"

The next part of creating your Facebook advertisement is going to be creating the Nicole content for the advertisement. The technical content includes you deciding who your advertisement is going to get seen by, including what their demographic as, what their interests are, and how likely they are to purchase from your company. Facebook will provide you with plenty of guidance to decide who you are going to show your advertisement to, but it is important that you already have a general understanding of who your target audience is. If you have not yet identified your target audience, it may be a good idea to avoid using paid promotions until you develop a clear understanding of who is following you on social media.

As you create your target audience on Facebook, you will notice that Facebook tells you approximately how many people are in your target audience. Facebook will also provide you with the opportunity to identify where are your sweet spot is, or how many people you should be targeting, by giving you a gauge of your audience. You will notice that in the center of the gauge on Facebook, there is a space that is green. You want to target the green space by ensuring that the parameters you include in your advertisement's directive, or technical information, lands you in the green space. If you are in the green space, you can ensure that you are targeting a healthy sized audience that will allow you to gain greater traction with your paid promotions.

Creating Your Ad "The Visual"

The next part of your advertisement that you are creating is known as "the visual." This part of your advertisement is responsible for creating the design, or what your audience is going to see when they see your paid promotion. You want to make sure that the visual creation for your advertisement is attractive to ensure that your audience is actually going to want to stop and pay attention to what you are sharing.

The visual content of your advertisement will include the words shared in your advertisement, the image that you choose to share, and the action that you want your audience to take when they see your promotion. It is important that you use written content that is relevant to your audience, and that provides them with some form of value to ensure that they are actually going to pay attention. In the past, using written content that was too long was ineffective as most people were not interested in actually reading what you had to share. These days, a lot of brands are gaining traction using longer pieces of written content; however they are ensuring that this content shares high-quality value that their audience is actually interested in paying attention to. Sharing this much free content in a paid promotion is actually a very valuable marketing strategy that you can use, as it shows your audience that you have plenty of information to share. In fact, it shows that you have so much to share that you can easily share large pieces of content for free because you have plenty of additional value to offer.

In addition to ensuring that the written content is high-quality, you also want to make sure that the image you are using is high-quality and relevant to your audience. Typically, using a high-quality or professionally photographed image is the best option. Many brands will use stock images. However, it is important that if you choose to use stock images, you refrain from using stock images that too many brands are using. If you use stock images that many brands are already using, it makes your brand look less genuine and prevents people from paying attention to you. Because so many brands are using stock images, your audiences used to see them already, and therefore they believe that you do not have anything authentic or genuine to share with them. A great way to bypass this problem if you do choose to use stock images is best to ensure that you are using a paid stock image website, that's ensuring that you are not using content that is already being used on a regular.

Lastly, you are going to need to choose what your call to action will be in your advertisement. Facebook provides plenty of call to action is already built into their advertisement feature, so all you need to do is choose one that is relevant to what your advertisement objective is. If you are unsure, consider what it is that you desire for your audience to do, and then choose the call to action that aligns with that.

Confirming Your Ad

Once your ad is created, all you need to do is confirm your advertisement. Facebook will review your advertisement to ensure that it meets their standards, as this is how they prevent inappropriate advertisements from getting promoted on their platform. Remember, Facebook is a site used by many people in many different age groups, so they do not want to have people sharing advertisements that contain inappropriate images or language.

After Facebook has approved your promotion, you will receive a message in your messenger confirming that it has been approved. Then, all you need to do is monitor the promotion. If within' 24-48 hours you do not feel that the post is creating the traction that you desire you can pause it. Then, you can simply create a new post to try again.

Boosted Posts

Boosted posts on Facebook are slightly different from traditional paid promotions. When you boost a post on Facebook, all you are doing is promoting a post that you have already created. In other words, if you have a post that is performing well on your Facebook page, you can boost that post so that it performs even better. Using boosted posts is a great opportunity for you to increase your organic reach, by adding a paid element.

In order to boost a post on Facebook, you will need to have an ad to manage your account already created. Once you have created the account, all you need to do is go to your Facebook business page, locate the post do you want to boost, and tap the boost button. Facebook will then allow you to determine who your target audience will be, how much you want to pay for the advertisement and launch the advertisement. They will then confirm your post, ensure that it meets their community standards, and then let you know that your post has been boosted. Then, just like with other paid promotion, you will want to monitor the impact of your boosted post to ensure that you are gaining the traction that you desire. If not, you can always end the promotion early. If it is, you can choose to add additional time to your promotion.

Chapter 5: Why Use Instagram?

Instagram is a powerful photograph sharing tool that can be used to connect with your audience through the power of image. When you use Instagram, your goal is to create a visual experience for your audience to follow. Brand to use Instagram as an opportunity to create a visual brand experience that allows their audience to create a personal relationship with the brand. If you choose to use Instagram as a part of your brand strategy, it is important that you focus on creating high-quality visual content for your audience. There are many ways that you can leverage Instagram to grow your business on social media, most of which we will discuss in this very chapter. From using stories to creating paid advertisements, you are going to discover how you can leverage Instagram to the fullest extent.

Organic Instagram Advertising

There are multiple ways in which you can organically advertise on Instagram. Some of these ways include Instagram stories, sharing pictures in your newsfeed, live videos, and direct messaging. Taking advantage of all of the different tools available to you on Instagram's platform is the best opportunity to leverage organic Instagram marketing to the fullest extent. Instagram stories, sharing pictures in your newsfeed, live videos, and direct messaging. Taking advantage of all of the different tools available to you on Instagram's platform is the best opportunity to leverage organic Instagram marketing to the fullest extent.

The biggest advantage of Instagram is that organic marketing platform allows you to produce a high volume of content for your audience for free. When you create organic Instagram advertising content, you establish a healthy platform of content for people to browse through when they discover you. For the people who already follow you, they are able to continue consuming excellent high-quality content through your Instagram platform, which results in them continuing to follow you for a long period of time. As with all social media platforms, people on Instagram preferred to follow and engage with accounts who are regularly creating content and sharing with their audience. For the people who already follow you, they are able to continue consuming excellent high-quality content through your Instagram platform, which results in them continuing to follow you for a long period of time. As with all social media platforms, people on Instagram prefer to follow and engage with accounts who are regularly creating content and sharing with their audience. The more you engage in the social aspect of social media, the more likely you were going to gain traction and develop your audience, which is especially true on Instagram.

The disadvantage to organic Instagram marketing is that it can take quite a long time to establish a healthy following. Many brands are seduced by the idea of buying followers as an opportunity to increase the apparent attraction behind their brand. Of course, the more followers you have, the easier it will be for you to attract new followers. However, if you did not organically earn your followers or earn them through paid Instagram promotions, then Instagram will stop showing your content to as many people. To Instagram, accounts who buy their followers are at risk of being spammy. As well, your true audience will see that you have a large following with very little engagement which leads to having fewer people take you seriously. As a result, you are less likely to be able to grow on the platform. So, the biggest drawback is that it will take you more time to grow and that you will need to be more strategic in growing your engagement well also a growing you're following. We will discuss how you can do both organic marketing and paid marketing on Instagram over the next few subsections.

Creating and Optimizing Your Instagram Profile

The first step in designing your organic Instagram strategy is creating and optimizing your Instagram profile. Creating an Instagram profile is simple, all you need to do is download the mobile application for Instagram to your phone and follow the step-by-step process of creating your profile. Once you have followed the steps to create the profile all you need to do is optimize that profile. To optimize the profile essentially means that you create a profile that is easy to identify, clear, and educational in terms of letting your audience know who they are looking at. Instagram enables you to use your username, your bio, people you. Instagram your link, and your images to create and optimize your profile.

When it comes to optimizing your username, it is important that you choose your brand name as your username. If you have a company name, this should be the username that you use. If you are running a personal brand, you can use your personal name on your username. Of course, it is important to understand that your user name may not be available on Instagram. For that reason, you need to understand how you can effectively differentiate your name without making yourself difficult to discover. So, the first and biggest thing that you need to understand when it comes to differentiating your name on Instagram is that you cannot do it using a series of numbers, strange spelling, or symbols. Adding these things to your user name can make it very challenging for people to identify you, thus resulting in you getting limited viewership. If you need to differentiate your name, the best way to do it is to add some other form of identifying marker. For example, many companies who share similar names will use their brand name followed by the name of the city in which the company is located to differentiate themselves from other companies with the same name.

Your bio is a very powerful tool on Instagram, using your bio to differentiate yourself by creating a clear image of who your brand is important. Your bio is your opportunity to explain who you are, what you do, why people should care, and how you were different from the other people who do what you do. As well, you only got 150 characters to create your bio. This means that you need to use these characters wisely and create a high-quality bio that provides a large amount of information interestingly. The best way to create a high-quality bio is to make sure that you use interesting words, words that are relevant to your audience into your brand, and anything that really sets you apart. For example, "just do it" is the slogan for the popular fitness company Nike, and of course, they use their slogan in their bio. This slogan differentiates the company by creating an identifiable reference point that they use across all of their branding messages. If you have a slogan, catchphrase, or any other message that you regularly share on other platforms, sharing that message in your bio is a great way to create brand recognition, while also setting yourself apart.

Every single Instagram platform has the opportunity to share a link in their profile. Taking advantage of this link to link to your website, to another social media platform, or even to your booking link is a great opportunity to funnel people from Instagram to your sales page. This way you can actually take advantage of Instagram as being a marketable feature because you are genuinely driving traffic to your sales links, thus increasing the amount of traffic you gain from Instagram. If you have multiple links you desire to share; you can always use a platform like Link Tree which is a valuable part from that allows you to share multiple links under one landing page. For some brands, providing the opportunity to find multiple different things through one convenient landing page is a valuable way to funnel people from Instagram to other areas in your business.

Finally, the next part of your Instagram platform that you need to optimize is the images. Below we will discuss how you can optimize your newsfeed. However you also need to understand that you have a profile picture which needs to be optimized. You can optimize your profile picture either by using a clear head shot, your company logo, or an image that is relevant to your brand. Refrain from using any images that have too much going on in them as this pain comes overwhelming and makes it challenging for your audience to understand who you are, and what you do. Keeping your profile picture clean, clear, and easy to understand makes it easier for people to identify whether or not are interested in your profile, and then whether they want to choose to follow you or not.

Designing Your Newsfeed

Your newsfeed is the area where you get the opportunity to share images of your company or images that are relevant to your company, with your audience. Designing your newsfeed in an attractive, interesting, and understandable manner is extremely important when it comes to leveraging Instagram as a marketable platform. These days, Instagram and visual marketing have been around for so long that the standards are high when it comes to producing visual content for a digital audience. You need to make sure that the images you are sharing are high-quality, that they look good next to each other, and that they make sense. If you have spent any time on I Instagram, chances are you have seen various newsfeeds that have a specific design to them. For example, many people will post one Image with a quote on it, then they will post a brand-related image, and then they will post another picture with a quote on it. They continue this pattern throughout their newsfeed, which produces a specific aesthetic for their page. Of course, you do not need to follow this exact style however it does give you a clear understanding of how Instagram design works.

In addition to having a pattern for how you are posting, you should also consider the color scheme that you are using on your profile. You will notice that most companies have a branded color scheme that they use on all of their online content. Having your own color scheme for Instagram, and any other online platform you are using is an excellent way to create consistency in your brand. You can choose any color scheme that you desire to use. However it is important that you choose colors that will appeal to your audience. So, for example, you are appealing to a classier audience, you would not want to be using several different bright, bold, and "out there" images on your platform, as this would not look classy. It is very important that you keep your brand consistent in order to ensure that you are leveraging brand recognition.

If you are ever unsure as to how you can design your newsfeed, a great tool to use is by going to your competitors' platforms and see how they are strategizing their content. After browsing a few of your competitors' pages, you will likely develop some inspiration for how you can design your own platform so that your page looks competitive as well. Remember, it is important that you do not directly copy your competition as this will prevent you from standing out from the crowd.

Hashtag Tips and Tricks

On Instagram, the way to get discovered is to use what is known as "hashtags." Hashtags are a way for people to search for content on Instagram, they work like keywords however they are designed slightly differently. In order to take advantage of a hashtag, you need to preface your keyword with a pound key symbol or this symbol "#." By creating hashtags for your content, you ensure that you are going to get found by your target audience. Of course, because hashtags work like keywords, it is important that you are using the right hashtags in order to get discovered. Below are a few great tips that you can use to get discovered with hashtags.

The first thing you need to do is identify what your niche is, and what keywords are relevant to your niche. So, if you are in the health and wellness industry, for example, your niche might be yoga. If yoga was your niche, you would want to be using hashtags that were relevant to yoga. You could start the process of discovering new yoga related hashtags by going to your Instagram application and typing in "#yoga" in the search bar. Once your search came up, you could begin discovering other people who were using this hashtag.

After landing on the search page that arises following searching for a niche specific hashtag on Instagram, there are two great ways for you to find high-quality hashtags that are relevant to your niche. First, you can start by looking at the "related" hashtags list to identify any hashtags that are regularly being used by people who are also searching for yoga. Then, you can look at people who are posting pictures similar to yours with the hashtag "#yoga" and see what other hashtags they are using.

In addition to making sure that you are discovering the right hashtags, you also need to make sure that you are disqualifying the wrong ones. On Instagram, it is not ideal to use any hashtags that are over 500,000 users as this can result in your content getting buried quickly. So, it is important that you look at the overall usage rating on every hashtag that you consider using to ensure it is not too large. You also want to refrain from using any that may be too generalized as you want to avoid having people who are not from your target audience seeing and following your content. Although there is nothing wrong with being followed by people who are not a part of your target audience, it does mean that these people are less likely to purchase from your company. Since you intend to use your Instagram platform to market, it is important that you look at it from a marketing perspective by targeting a very specific audience, particularly through your usage of hashtags.

Engaging with Your Followers

The final, and potentially most important step when it comes to marketing organically on Instagram is engaging with your followers. You can engage with your followers by creating stories on your profile, and using this as an opportunity to give behind the scenes insight into your brand. You can engage with your followers by commenting back when they comment on your content. You can engage with your followers by liking and commenting on their content. You can even engage with your followers by sending them a direct message thanking them for their support. There are many ways that you can engage with your audience to create a more engaging and enjoyable experience for your audience by nurturing your relationship with them.

Remember, putting the social back into social media is a very big trend right now. People are leaning towards brands, companies, influencers, and other people who are actually taking the time to engage. If you are not taking the time to engage with your audience on Instagram, there is a good chance that they may lose interest in you and stop following you. If you want to build a positive reputation, and a great, engaged following on social media you need to take advantage of engaging back with your audience.

Paid Instagram Marketing

Paid Instagram marketing works just like Facebook marketing. Like with Facebook marketing, you will use the Facebook ads manager to manage your Instagram advertisements. So, everything you did to create a Facebook advertisement would also be done to create an Instagram advertisement. In fact, you can actually create advertisements that run both on Facebook and Instagram at the same time allowing you to integrate both platforms and get the most out of your money.

If you want to advertise exclusively on Instagram, you can simply create the advertisement on the Facebook ads manager and then choose to only run that advertisement on Instagram. The only prerequisite for you to be able to do those is that you link your Instagram account to a Facebook business page. As long as your Instagram is linked to a Facebook Page, you will be able to run your Instagram advertisements through the Facebook ads manager.

Types of Instagram Advertisements

There are four different types of paid Instagram advertisements that you can use. The first type of Instagram advertisement you can use looks like a simple Instagram post but is boosted so that a broader range of people can see it.

The second type of Instagram advertisement that you can use is known as a carrousel advertisement and allows you to share multiple photographs. It is common for people to use carrousel advertisements as an opportunity to show off multiple products on one single advertisement. For example, large makeup companies will share multiple deals on one single boosted post and all their audience has to do is swipe through the various pictures to see what the latest deals are.

The third type of advertisement you can do is similar to a standard post. However it uses a video instead of just a photograph. This is similar to an advertisement that you might watch on TV, or YouTube, as it provides you with the opportunity to leverage paid video marketing. Many brands will use this as an opportunity to show off their products, give an idea of what their services are all about, or create a unique brand message based on video content.

The final type of paid advertisement you can use on Instagram is fairly new, and it exists within the story feed. Instagram recently introduced the ability to pay to have your advertisement seen between stories. So, anytime someone is watching their friends story feed your advertisement may pop up in between stories. These video advertisements last for 15 seconds or less and give you the opportunity to turn more attention to your brand.

Chapter 6: Why Use Google?

Many people are unaware of the fact that you can leverage Google as an advertising platform. On Google, you can share boosted posts, paid advertisements, and even use organic SEO strategies to get found. Although Google itself is not technically a social media platform, it does integrate with most of the major platforms which makes it a very valuable tool to use. In this chapter, you are going to discover how you can take advantage of Google to help your business get found online, grow your social media platform, and increase the number of sales that you are bringing in through the internet. By learning how to leverage Google effectively, you can ensure that you are growing as quickly as possible and that you are making the most of your time spent online.

Organic Google Advertising

Organically building your presence on Google starts by understanding one very key marketing strategy on this search engine. This key marketing strategy is known as "search engine optimization." Search engine optimization, or SEO, is a powerful backend tool that you can use to rank higher on search engines. You can integrate SEO strategies into all of the platforms that you use.

The biggest benefit of taking advantage of organic Google marketing is that it allows you to rank higher on Google search results without having to pay. So, anytime someone goes to Google and searches for a company like yours if your SEO is effective you will be discovered. If your SEO is ineffective, you will rank lower, which means that fewer people will find you and you will be less likely to get discovered.

There truly aren't many drawbacks to organic Google marketing. Of course, if you pay Google you can rank higher without having to put in the SEO work. However it is still a good idea to continue doing it anyway so that you can rank better and better. As a result, everyone should be taking advantage of using Google's organic marketing strategies.

SEO

SEO is a strategy that can be used on virtually every platform that you spend time on. However, the biggest place where you want to be taking advantage of SEO is on your company website so that your website can rank higher. That being said, the more you incorporate SEO into your all-around online presence, the more likely you will be to get discovered online. You should be mindful of SEO practices for every piece of content that you create and share online so that you can begin growing your brand as quickly as possible.

The biggest and most effective SEO tool that is available is keywords. Keywords are basically popular search terms that your audience is most likely to look up in order to discover brands who offer products or services just like yours. Every niche has multiple keywords that can be used to help customers find relevant content, so it is important that you familiarize yourself with the ones that are relevant to your niche. You can do this by using any keyword finding tool, such as Google Keywords, to discover what keywords are relevant to your niche. Once you have located them, you want to use them as much as is naturally possible on your online platform so that your accounts and website are all associated with this keyword.

It is important that you refrain from overusing keywords, however, as most search engines perceive the overuse of keywords to mean that the platform is filled with spam or low-quality content. Keeping keywords to 2-3% of your overall content is ideal to ensure that your platform is associated with the keyword but not ignored as being potential spam.

In addition to keywords, alt text is important. Adding alt text to your photographs on your website, to your Instagram and Facebook images, and other parts of your platform is a good way to make sure that you are getting discovered by your audience. Alt text is essentially a text-based title for your images that allows people on various devices to read what your images are about. Not only does it make your platform more user-friendly, but it also helps you add more keywords into your platform.

Paid Google Advertising

Advertising on Google is a powerful opportunity to get your business in front of a large audience fairly quickly. When you advertise on Google, you not only get seen by a larger audience faster, but you can also get seen across multiple platforms. Google offers what is known as pay per click or PPC advertising options, which essentially means that any time someone actually clicks on your advertisement you pay. These PPC advertisements are placed on the search engine platform itself, as well as on other websites that have Google ads enabled, such as many blogs and informational websites.

Accessing Ad Manager

Creating an ad account with Google requires you to log into Google AdWords. If you do not yet have an AdWords account, you can easily create one by navigating to the AdWords account on your desktop and creating an account. You will be walked through the process of inputting some personal information into the platform in order to validate your account. Once you have created the AdWords account, you will simply need to head to the "Create Ad" tab in the actions menu and begin creating your new Google Advertisement. You will have the option of deciding how your ad will be displayed so that you can get seen by your target audience.

Creating Your Ad "Behind the Scenes"

Once you have opened up the option to create a new ad, you will need to create the behind the scenes content first. You will start by setting your bid on the ad so that you can determine how much you are willing to spend overall, and how much you are willing to spend per click. In advertising terms, those who are willing to spend the most per click will have priority placement whereas those who are not will have a lower priority when it comes to ad placement. That being said, even a lower budget will still get you seen as long as you create the right advertisement for your audience.

Once you have set the bid, you will need to pay attention to your quality score. On Google, a quality score is basically a score that Google gives you that determines whether or not your ad is relevant for what people are searching and how high quality the advertisement is. For Google, they want to be showing advertisements that are relevant, most likely to be clicked, and most likely to serve the customers' needs. By favoring high-quality advertisements, they keep clients happy and increase the value of ad space, which means that the service will continue to be made available. You can increase your quality score by using clear and concise descriptors of who you are and what you have to offer so that Google knows exactly who to show your ad to.

Creating Your Ad "The Visual"

The final part of creating your Google ad is creating the visual. The visual for Google ads are limited: you are often kept only to your link, a title, and a description. Depending on where the ad will be placed, you may also get the opportunity to include an image with your ad. That being said, the biggest part of your "visual" is going to extend beyond the ad itself. For the ad, clear and interesting words are plenty. The second part is having a high quality, relevant, and attractive landing page for your audience to discover. This way, when your lead clicks on your link and lands on your page, they are immediately interested in what they see, and they are more likely to stay on your page rather than leaving it right away and never considering your company again.

You can either hire a designer to create the landing page for you, or you can create it for yourself. If you want to create it for yourself and you are not exactly tech-savvy, you can always use a platform like Squarespace, Mail Chimp, or Kajabi to create a landing page for your audience to land on. These click and create platforms are excellent for having your audience land on a high quality and functional landing page that can also lead them through a sales funnel. Plus, they support you in creating consistent and high-quality designs which makes it easier for you to have high-quality pages that will create a higher aesthetic appeal for your audience.

Chapter 7: Why Use Twitter?

Twitter is a platform that many have questioned for years: some people get it, and others don't. The ones who get it typically fall in love with the platform immediately and find it to be highly valuable for their audience. Others find themselves struggling to navigate the platform at all and wonder if it is even worth it to keep their brand on the platform. Of course, where you spend time is entirely up to you, but if your brand is catering to the target audience that exists on Twitter, getting on Twitter is likely a good idea. Twitter is one of the only platforms that cater to the middle-age demographic, which can make it a very valuable asset if you do as well.

Getting on Twitter and figuring it out does not have to be hard. In fact, it can be fun and easy while also creating great traction for you in the social media world since the link click-through rates on Twitter are over 80%! That means that you have a high potential for getting people to visit your profile and then click through to your audience to begin shopping from your brand! If you are ready to learn how to tap into that audience, this chapter will tell you exactly how you can do just that.

Organic Twitter Advertising

Organic Twitter advertising is similar to other platforms: the more you post and engage the more brand recognition you will receive and the greater your organic marketing reach will be. The thing with Twitter is that most of your marketing will be organic as it provides you with the best opportunity to really create relationships with your audience. Twitter itself revolves around having conversations with groups of people, which means that conversation is your most powerful asset on Twitter. You will learn how to get into the conversation later, but you should know that this is going to be your biggest growth tool on Twitter.

The advantage to Twitter is that the majority of marketing on this platform takes place for free. The more you engage in conversations or, better yet, start conversations the better. So, all you need to do is join in on the conversation, and you will be making waves. Once you figure out the learning curve of how the conversation works on Twitter, you will likely discover that this is extremely easy to do, which will allow you to have greater success on Twitter. As well, as you continue engaging in these conversations, you have a powerful opportunity to position your brand by making your brands' opinion on various niche-specific conversations well known. This can help you add a greater "personality" to your brand so that people can reflect and resonate with you, even more, allowing you to grow faster and create deeper connections and relationships with your audience.

The disadvantage of marketing on Twitter is that the platform does tend to take up a lot of time in order for you to stay engaged in the conversation. The more you use it and start conversations, the more you will need to check in to see how those conversations are going and continually add your opinion in so that you stay relevant. As soon as you stop commenting, you slowly fade away in the conversation and people may be less likely to see and find you.

Creating and Optimizing Your Twitter Profile

The key to converting on Twitter is creating and optimizing your profile. Since Twitter has such a high number of click-throughs, you want to make sure that you are creating an attractive profile that encourages people to actually want to click through on your links. You can do this by creating an informational and interesting bio, adding your link, and using a profile picture and header image that will personalize your profile.

Your bio on Twitter should be direct and interesting. You should immediately tell people who you are and what you do while adding in a flair of your brand's personality in just a few words. For example, "Sassy Mom blogger who loves cheese." Or "Natural clothing company with #hippievibes." Keeping your bio direct and personal ensures that people immediately know who you are and what you offer from the moment that they land on your page.

Many people on Twitter will use their header image to promote themselves, too, by adding a few words about themselves or an image of their latest product or service. You can leverage your profile header, too, by using an application like Canva to customize an image that shares a word or two about your latest service or product. Doing so will allow people to see your header as an attractive advertisement of sorts from the moment that they land on your profile, which may further compel them to check out your link, too.

Getting Your Page Verified

Getting verified on Twitter is simple, and it also distinguishes your profile by adding a certain level of credibility that does not exist on accounts that have not yet been verified. There are three steps that you will need to take to get your account verified. You will also need to make sure that your account type is actually eligible for verification, as Twitter will not immediately grant verification to just anyone. Twitter will grant verification status to accounts that revolve around:

- Politics
- Theatre or Film
- Fashion
- Music
- Journalism or Media
- Sports
- Public Interest
- Business or Companies
- Celebrities (to ensure people are not following imposters and celebrities are not becoming victims of identity theft.)

As long as you fit into these categories, you can follow these three steps to get verified on Twitter:

1. Prepare your account by ensuring that your avatar or profile image is of your actual face or your business logo. Twitter will not verify accounts that are using unidentifiable or irrelevant avatars as this

makes the account seem fake or spammy. You also need to use your real name or real business name, add a link to your website, set your account to public, and create a clear and easy to understand bio. Twitter will look at all of these things to verify that your account is real.

2. Twitter will request some information to support you in validating your account. First, they want to know why you want to have your account verified, so you will need to give a letter of intent. You will also need to provide identification to prove that you are who you say you are, and if necessary, you will need to provide links that demonstrate that you are who you say you are online.

3. Finally, you will need to go to "verification.twitter.com/request" and fill out the form to request verification. This is how you will send all of the relevant information to Twitter and begin the process of getting verified. If they approve you, it will be notified to you through this message. If they do not, it will be

explained in this thread as well and, if necessary, you can make the adjustments required to complete the verification process.

Using Video Marketing on Twitter

Unlike Facebook and Instagram, Twitter does not have a story feed that you can use. However, they do allow you to upload videos to your page to be watched. Studies show that Twitter users respond better to videos that are created and then uploaded versus those that are filmed live or within the app, as most viewers want to see end-to-end, they do not want to watch how the story unfolds. Knowing that creating a Twitter video strategy is quite easy, you just need to create a strategy that allows you to create videos beforehand and then upload them into the application.

The best way to create videos for Twitter is to decide which type of content you want to film, film the videos in advance, and then upload them to Twitter. Videos that are five minutes or less will work best on this platform, so keep your videos short and direct. You can film on almost any subject, from entertaining to educational, so choose that which fits your brand the best and start there! Make sure that the film you create is high quality, not pixelated, and that it has great lighting so that people can easily see you and stay focused. The higher quality the visuals and audio are for your film; the more people will be likely to watch it.

Having A Post Schedule

Because Twitter is such a busy application that can easily drain a significant amount of your time and energy, having a posting schedule can be a helpful way to avoid getting lost on Twitter. You can create a Twitter posting schedule by choosing two to three times per day where you would like to upload something to Twitter and then post at those times. You can then spend some time engaging with your audience following that post and then leave Twitter alone entirely so that you do not spend too much time on the app.

Alternatively, you can create Tweets and then schedule them out ahead of time so that you are not required to post multiple times a day. You can do this directly in the Twitter app by going to the "Creatives" tab, clicking "New Tweet" and then scheduling the Tweet in advance before posting it. If you choose to post on this form of schedule, all you will need to do is head onto Twitter once or twice a day to engage with your audience and respond to any engagement that you may have received so that you can keep the momentum going. The more your momentum builds, the better, which means that you will have an easier time growing your account.

Taking Advantage of Twitter Teams

If you are running a larger business or if you have people who can help you run your online business, Twitter team is a great opportunity to run your business account with more than one person. Twitter teams can be created through logging into the TweetDeck and then tapping the "Accounts" tab in the navigation menu.

From there, you can add accounts to your Twitter team who can support you in running your business online. Once you have authorized team members, they can help you by answering direct messages, posting Tweets, or replying to Tweets. This can be helpful for businesses who have larger teams or where the person running the business (you) is hands-off in the social media end of things. By having your account set to host teams, you can gain support in running your account, and you can take some of the pressure off yourself.

Getting Involved in the Conversation

Twitter is reliant on conversation as it is built entirely around conversing with people through large threads. In order to get out there and build connections, you need to get involved in the conversation or, better yet, start the conversation. You can do this by looking for relevant Tweets in your newsfeed and responding to those Tweets to get involved in the conversation. The best way to do this is to go to trending Tweets on your home page, find the

Tweets that are relevant to your niche, and then begin responding to people in the thread! It may look confusing at first, but as you grow more aware of how it works, it will become easier and more enjoyable for you to engage.

Posting Relevant Content

Another way to get in on the conversation is to post relevant content. It is important that you post relevant organic content and that you retweet relevant content in order to get found on Twitter. Ideally, when you repost content, you should look to repost content that is getting higher engagement as this is content that is already performing well so you can use it to leverage your own account. Make sure that the content you retweet, reply to, and post is all relevant and on-brand as it can all be seen from your profile so you do not want to have irrelevant or negative content being shared on your account as this can dilute the quality of your brand.

Paid Twitter Advertising

Many people are surprised to learn that paid advertising on Twitter is actually highly effective. When you use it, you have the capacity to reach a large audience fairly quickly. The biggest disadvantage to paid marketing on Twitter is that you can get missed by your audience very easily if you do not target your audience correctly. As well, many larger companies are on Twitter so if you are not targeting and budgeting effectively your advertisements may not work as the advertisements being purchased by larger companies will be more likely to get seen.

Twitter Analytics

The first thing you need to do when it comes to creating a Twitter advertisement is look at your analytics. You can begin measuring your analytics by checking out your Tweet Activity Dashboard. There, you will locate analytics of every single Tweet that you have ever made on your Twitter account. Next, you can look at your "Audience Insights Dashboard" which will enable you to get a clear look into who your audience is on Twitter. Remember, you are likely going to attract different segments of your target audience on different platforms, so it is important that you look into your Twitter specific audience when you start creating Twitter advertisements rather than simply using the target audience that you may have already formulated for your general business plan.

When you look at these two metrics, you are going to find out two very important pieces of information about your audience: what types of content people like the most and who is following your content. With this information, you can formulate Tweets that are going to be on par with the ones that your audience is already consuming and target those Tweets directly to the audience who is most likely to see them and take action. You will want to keep track of this information as this is your key opportunity to produce Twitter advertisements that will actually produce results for you.

Setting Your Objective

After you have discovered what your Tweet needs to look like, you need to set what your objective is. Twitter provides you with four different objectives on Twitter: raise awareness of a specific Tweet, drive traffic to your website, attract new followers to your account, or increase the engagement that you are receiving on your account. You need to make sure that you choose the objective that is most aligned with your goals, so pick the one that fits your needs. If you are not entirely sure as to which one that will be, you can always do split testing by running two similar advertisements with different objectives and appearances and seeing which one gets you the best return on your investment.

Picking Your Audience

Next, you need to identify your audience. Here, as long as you have already looked at your analytics, the process is simple. All you need to do is outline your target audience, upload that information into the Twitter ad creative, and hit confirm. You will have the opportunity to determine which gender you want to target, from what geographical area, what interests they may have, and who they may already be following online. This last option: who your target audience may be following on Twitter, is particularly important as it allows you to target people who are already following your competition which is a great qualifier when it comes to determining who is going to be a hot lead for your business.

Paying for Your Ad

Next, you need to pay for your ad. Paying for your ad on Twitter is slightly different than paying on other platforms as you will set both an overall budget *and* a maximum budget of what you want to be paying per engagement. This way, rather than having to set a budget and potentially having that budget spent on high bid engagements, you can instead have it spent on the ones that are going to serve your business best. If you are not entirely sure as to what bidding price you want to pay per engagement, you can always choose twitters automatic billing tool which will determine the best bed cost based on your budget, your goals, and your industry. After you have set your budget, all you need to do is confirm your budget and input your payment method.

Creating Your Ad

Lastly, you are going to need to design the creative for your ad! There are a few key things that you want to consider when it comes to creating your advertisement on Twitter. First, you need to think about the written content that you are going to be using for your advertisement. Ideally, you want to use content that is going to be captivating, and that will have a strong call to action to encourage your users to engage with the goal of your advertisement. You want to avoid using hashtags (#) or mentions (@) on your advertisement as this can result in people clicking away from your ad and never taking you up on your call to action. Naturally, this works against the objective of your goal which makes it not ideal.

Twitter themselves recommend having 4 to 5 Tweets that you will boost your campaign to ensure that you gain maximum visibility and reach, so designing a few Tweets may be ideal. If you choose to run a campaign with multiple Tweets, make sure that you design each Tweet to be unique and that you always target the same audience. This way, the people who see your advertisements are likely to continue seeing all of them, and they will be able to recall your brand easier with each Tweet. As a result, you gain both brand recognition and an increased chance of having your objective met with each lead. If you do choose to run multiple advertisements, make sure you split your overall budget up evenly amongst each of the advertisements that you run to avoid going over. Twitter will not do this for you, so it is important that you do it for yourself to avoid being charged four or five times more than what you expected to pay for your advertisements.

Chapter 8: Why Use YouTube?

YouTube was one of the original platforms to support people in generating massive traction through their online brand. YouTube, alongside Instagram, presented a platform for the rise of influencers who are now responsible for driving the world of online business. Getting on YouTube is an excellent way to get involved in video marketing while also creating a platform for you to share content with your audience on the net. Whether you choose to grow your YouTube channel as a primary platform or if you choose to grow your YouTube channel as an opportunity to share videos across other platforms as well, there are many ways that you can weave YouTube into your overall marketing strategy online.

It is important to understand that YouTube is different from other platforms as it operates more like a search engine for videos than an actual social media site. When you get on YouTube, you need to be prepared to allow yourself the opportunity to embrace the learning curve as you learn to leverage YouTube like a true marketing strategy, rather than simply getting on it and getting lost in the shuffle. Once you embrace the strategy for growth on

YouTube, you will likely discover that it is a powerful place for you to massively grow your business and establish authority in the online space.

Organic YouTube Marketing

Organic marketing on YouTube is simple and, due to the nature of the platform, it can also be easy to draw large amounts of traffic over to your YouTube channel which can help your channel grow faster. Since the entire purpose of YouTube is to create videos and have other people watch them, you will benefit best if you create videos that are high quality, relevant, and engaging to keep people interested in watching your content. You will learn more about how you can do that later in this very chapter!

The biggest advantage of organic YouTube marketing is that you can get a lot of traction when it comes to sharing your content on YouTube. Unlike other platforms where you are likely to simply sink beneath everyone else's posts and get lost if you are not doing it right, on YouTube you can share your videos around and leverage the audience that you have already built elsewhere online. As a result, you can grow your audience faster, get seen by more people quicker, and increase your ranking ratings on YouTube's SEO platform. This means that with YouTube, you can really make big waves in a quick timeframe, especially if you already have a larger audience in other areas on the internet.

The disadvantage to organic YouTube marketing is that if you do not already have a large audience elsewhere, it can be more challenging for you to generate an audience within the YouTube app itself. Although it is certainly possible, it will take you more time to generate your audience so that you can market your videos to a larger number of people. Additionally, many people are on YouTube making content so it can be more challenging to make content that is authentic and unique from what already exists online. That being said, if you take the time to look into your brands' authentic message and work toward differentiating yourself by creating a unique brand personality, this can be easier to overcome.

Creating and Optimizing Your YouTube Channel

The first thing that you need to do in order to begin creating a powerful YouTube presence is creating and optimizing your channel. You can easily create a YouTube channel by going to YouTube.com and clicking "Create Channel." Once you have, you will be given the option to create a channel for yourself, or your business. Make sure that you click the business option so that you can customize the name of your channel, as personal accounts cannot customize their channel names. Then, you will be walked through the process of naming your channel and setting up your account. After you have followed the prompts, the basic structure of your channel will be complete, and all you will need to do is optimize your channel so that you can increase your chances of being found and followed by your target audience.

The first step that you should use to optimize your channel is to fill out the "about" section on your page so that you can give potential viewers an opportunity to learn more about who you are, what you offer, and how they can learn more about your business. Often, companies will link to their website through their about me page, or they will share their email address so that you can directly get in touch with them, depending on the structure and size of the company. You should take advantage of putting this information in your *about* section as well to ensure that anyone who is interested in learning more about your business or doing business with you.

On your channel, you will notice that you have a settings menu that allows you to go into your advanced settings, where you can adjust various things. One setting you will want to adjust is your channel's keyword tags so that your channel is more likely to show up under certain keywords. When you choose to set up these keywords, or meta tags, you will have 100 characters to highlight what your channel is about. It is important that you use these keywords wisely and that they are actually relevant to your channel so that you are more likely to get found. You can always use Google Keywords here to identify what your niche's keywords are most likely to be so that you can use the keywords that are going to gain you the most traction on your website.

Lastly, you will want to add a trailer to your channel. On YouTube, you can film a short introductory video that is displayed on the main page of your profile which automatically begins to show your followers who you are and what you are all about. You want your trailer to be interesting, captivating, branded, and relevant to what your channel will be all about so that when people land on your page, they feel informed and clear on what to expect. If your trailer is filmed properly, you can feel confident that it will pique people's interest in not only our channel but also in your brand, so take the time to make sure that it is high quality, interesting, and engaging. If you are unsure of how you can structure your trailers channel, consider going to other channels that are similar to yours and check out what they have done to create trailers for their own channels. Draw inspiration from theirs by highlighting what you like most about each trailer and then go ahead and begin filming your own. Once you have, upload it to your channel as your trailer so that everyone can see it and fall in love with your channel right away.

Filming YouTube Videos

Since film is the entire purpose of YouTube, knowing how to create high-quality films is important if you are going to help your channel grow and create the traction that you desire. On YouTube, you want to make sure that your videos are longer so that you can increase your viewer retention and maximize your potential of getting found online. On YouTube, one of the biggest metrics they pay attention to is average channel watch time as this allows them to determine whether or not your channel is relevant and interesting to their audience. The higher your watch time minutes are, the more likely you will be seen over anyone else, thus allowing your channel to grow and become more popular.

You also want to make sure that you are keeping your films high quality, as virtually everyone on the internet these days has high-quality cameras to film with, and you need to remain competitive. Ideally, you should be shooting everything in 4k. However you can get away with filming in 1080p. You should refrain from going any lower as all devices are starting to become 4k enabled, meaning that people are going to favor higher quality resolutions in videos, so if you are not filming in higher resolution you might lose audience members over this. In addition to having a high-resolution camera, you also want to have high-quality lighting so that your videos are properly illuminated. Like with having high-resolution video quality, having high-quality lighting is also important as your audience will not want to be watching a video where they can hardly see what you are doing or make out the contents of the video itself.

In addition to the equipment that you are using, you also want to make sure that what you are filming is high quality and interesting, too. You can start by improving your on-camera skills through speaking more clearly and in an audible tone, being very direct and confident in what you are saying, and sitting comfortably yet confidently with your body pointed toward the camera. These basic camera skills will improve your ability to create high-quality videos which will, in turn, increase your ability to get located since it will result in more people paying attention to your channel.

The next part of creating high-quality videos is having something interesting to share with your audience so that they have a reason to pay attention to your films. Make sure that you are very clear in your purpose so that everyone can easily understand what your video is about and what information can be gained from that specific video. This will not only keep your video relevant and interesting, but it will also make it easier for you to title it and describe it to everyone who may be interested in watching the video. So, if you were talking about nutrition, for example, you would want to pick a very specific part of nutrition and talk about that in your video without straying off topic to talk about anything else. Perhaps you wanted to talk about prenatal nutrition, for example, you would want to make sure that everything you talked about was very specific to prenatal nutrition. You may feel inspired to go off topic and start talking about newborn nutrition or toddler nutrition if it interests you, but the reality is that this will simply make your video unclear and difficult to follow which will reduce your viewership. Instead, you want to pay attention to your specific topic, flow through the video with an introduction, the information, and a conclusion, and then end your video. This way, it is clear, direct, and to-the-point.

Lastly, you might want to consider having a professional introduction made for your videos. Many avid YouTube folks share their content with a unique introductory clip that distinguishes their channel from any others. You can think of this as being the same as the introduction clip to your favorite show on cable TV: complete with some graphics and a song in the background. Having this type of introduction clip on your video makes your brand memorable and helps people identify who you are right away, not only on YouTube but on the internet in general. You can easily get an introductory clip made for $30-$500 through a freelancer which can be located on a site like Fiverr.

Marketing Your Videos

Lastly, you will need to market your videos! You can market your videos on YouTube by sharing them on as many different networks as possible. For example, you can share it with a blurb to YouTube and Twitter, you can embed the video on your website, and you can share it in an email newsletter when your new video goes out each week, or every few days. You can also share a clip in your Instagram and Facebook stories so that everyone gets to see your content and get a sample of what you are sharing on YouTube. Make sure that you always link to the video so that people can easily find it and get their eyes on your new video without having to go hunt for it. If you require your audience to go hunt it down, chances are they will not waste their time looking for it at all. You should also make sure that every time you share videos you encourage people to share your video with someone who will be likely to enjoy your content. This way, not only do you get in front of your existing audience but you increase your chances of being shared to their friends, too, thus allowing your channel to grow even faster.

You can also market your channel in general by linking to it around the net. For example, if you use a Link Tree landing page on Instagram you can link to it there, you can add your link to Twitter, put it on your website, and even place it at the bottom of your emails. You can also remind people from time to time that you run a YouTube channel and that they can subscribe to your channel for great video content by occasionally sharing about it online. The more you talk about your channel and your videos, the more people are going to discover you on

YouTube and, therefore, the more likely you will be to get found.

Paid YouTube Marketing

YouTube has two ways that you can leverage paid marketing: having your clip show up before a video starts, or having your video boosted in the search results for certain keyword searches. You can create either style of campaign on YouTube by logging into your Google AdWords account and selecting the option to advertise on YouTube, as Google manages YouTube's marketing features. Once you are on this platform and ready to go, you can follow the steps below to get your advertisement live!

Measuring YouTube Analytics

First, you want to measure your YouTube analytics so that you can get a feel for what your audience prefers to receive from you on YouTube. If you have a specific objective for your videos, such as getting people to buy a certain product or service, you will want to pay attention to what structure of video is most popular on your channel. For example, do people respond best when you are entertaining and lighthearted, or do they respond best when you are serious and teaching them in a class-type setting? Understanding how your audience prefers to receive content is the best way to make sure that you are creating content that your audience will be most likely to pay attention to and receive. You also want to pay attention to who your demographic is, how long they are watching your content for, and any other highlights you may see in your analytics. The more you pay attention to what your audience is willing to receive, the easier it will be for you to create content that will target your audience more effectively so that your advertisement is actually productive.

Choosing Your Objective

Next, you need to determine what your objective is going to be for your advertisement, or what goal you have with your advertisement. You can choose any objective that fits your needs the best, whether it be getting more people to subscribe to your channel or getting more people to land on your website so that they can buy your products. Once you have your objective in mind, you will want to create your entire advertisement around that objective, from choosing what content you are going to film to determining how you are going to share that content with your audience so that they can pay attention to your channel.

Filming Your Advertisement

Next, you need to actually film your advertisement. If you only plan on sponsoring a video that you have already created, this part will be easy. All you need to do is upload that particular video into your AdWords account and select it as being the video that you will sponsor or boost so that it gets seen higher in the search rankings. Or, to be more specific, at the top of the search rankings so that people see you before anyone else when they search for videos that are relevant to the one that you are boosting.

If you are going to promote a video that is going to be seen embedded inside of someone else's videos, you will want to make sure that you are filming a high-quality video that is going to help people feel inspired to actually pay attention to the video that you are promoting. You will need to use all of the filming tips from earlier in this chapter but really take the quality and engagement of your film to the next level in order to ensure that your video gets traction as you promote it. If you do not create an extremely high-quality video, chances are you are not going to have your audience watch all the way through which will result in you wasting your time and money on this promotion.

Here is where you can combine your analytics and objective to design a video that will clearly target what your audience wants and needs. You can use the data you collected from your analytics to determine what format your video should be in and what trends or traits you need to bring into the video to make it interesting for your target audience to pay attention to. As you do, make sure that you are very clear about what it is that you are promoting so that people know exactly what it is that they are watching on your channel. If you pay attention to these important elements of your ad directive, you will discover that it can be really simple to turn high results from paid YouTube marketing.

Creating Your Campaign

Creating your campaign in the backend on AdWords takes a bit of practice, but it is not challenging to do. First, you are going to have to determine how much you want to pay for your advertisement or what your overall budget is. For YouTube promotions, you can choose both your daily budget and your budget per view to ensure that you are getting the maximum results from your promotion. If you are not entirely sure as to what you should be paying per view, you can always allow Google to automatically set the bid rates for you. The average view should cost between $0.01 and $0.23, and you will only pay this rate if someone watches your advertisement all the way through. Google will not charge you if they skip your advertisement to get ahead in the video.

Next, you need to set up your demographic so that Google knows who to target with your video, which ultimately allows them to determine which videos your video will appear in. For example, if you have an audience who loves cooking and your channel is about recipes, Google and YouTube will target other cooking-based channels to avoid having your recipe video show up in yoga videos or anywhere else. This way, your content is seen by relevant people, and YouTube does not lose retention for placing advertisements in odd areas on their platform. The demographic that you outline should match the one highlighted in your metrics, as these are the individuals who have already shown that they are the most interested in watching your videos and consuming your content. Avoid trying to make up your own metrics or analytics for this as you may end up guessing wrong and wasting a significant amount of money in your advertisements.

Finally, you need to upload your video to AdWords and then click "Confirm." Google will then proof your video to ensure that there is no nudity, swearing, or other inappropriate content being shared on the advertisement. If there is, they will decline your video and request that you change it so that the platform stays friendly for viewers of all ages. If there is nothing that goes against YouTube's community guidelines, then your video will be approved and will begin getting seen on YouTube within 24 hours. After that time frame, you will be able to pay attention to YouTube's analytics so that you can see how your advertisement is performing and whether or not it is generating the results that you desire. If it is, you can continue to let the ad perform so that you can get your positive conversions from your promotion! If it is not, you can pause the advertisement or end it early to avoid having to pay money for an advertisement that is underperforming.

Chapter 9: Why Use LinkedIn?

LinkedIn is another online marketing tool that is popular in the professional world. In fact, LinkedIn is the leading B2B social media platform in the world right now. LinkedIn allows professionals to upload a virtual resume of sorts to their profile so that they can showcase their skills and talents and connect with other professionals in the online space. Being on LinkedIn is a great way to make sales, find people to collaborate with, and grow in general so that you can begin experiencing greater results from your social media marketing strategies.

Many people are unaware of the value of LinkedIn because they have not been properly educated on how to use it, which results in them avoiding it altogether. Furthermore, LinkedIn is very niche-specific in that it truly only caters for B2B connections so unless you are marketing to professionals specifically, you will be unlikely to get as many results from your efforts on LinkedIn as you may desire. In other words, if you are not marketing to businesses or business professionals, LinkedIn may not be the best platform for you. If you are, however, LinkedIn can be a powerful tool to plug you directly into a world of professionals who can support you in growing and expanding for greater reach and greater conversions through your social media audience. If this sounds like the type of audience you are looking for, you will discover exactly how to leverage LinkedIn in this chapter.

Organic LinkedIn Marketing

Organic marketing on LinkedIn works similar to organic marketing on Facebook: you will make status updates, share images and articles, upload videos, and share other relevant content with your audience. You will also want to engage back and forth with your audience to make sure that you are getting seen and that you are investing in the process of building relationships with them so that your audience comes to know who you are. The process of building relationships on LinkedIn is important as this supports you in getting seen, building a reputation, and nurturing your connection with your existing audience. It is important that you realize that, similar to Twitter, LinkedIn will show all of your followers what you have been liking and engaging with so anything you engage with on LinkedIn is not private. You can leverage this by liking and engaging with things that are relevant to your industry, as this helps grow your presence with more content that is on-brand.

The advantage to organic LinkedIn marketing is very obvious: you get directly in front of a curated audience who will be interested in doing business with your brand. You can easily leverage your skills and endorsements from other professionals on the platform so that your audience can see what you are good at and what you are known for and quickly qualify or disqualify you for what they are looking for. In this way, you can use LinkedIn similarly to an online resume that can help you link up with potential clients or collaborators who can support you in further growth. As well, LinkedIn is a very growth-based platform where virtually everyone on it wants to connect with people and discover how they can support them in growing as a professional. In this sense, it supports you in creating a positive element of growth in your business.

Marketing on LinkedIn is especially valuable for B2B service professionals who work directly with their clients, such as hiring agencies, virtual assistants, and consultants. Because you have the opportunity to establish relationships with the people who are most likely to hire you on this social networking platform, it becomes easy for you to get your name out there, build a reputation for yourself, and become memorable to others. Through this form of online branding, it becomes easier for you to get your name out there and share with the people who are most likely to work with your business, and become identifiable to them. Because you are not only advertising yourself, but you are also building a reputation and relationships, you become memorable to the point where your audience will likely think of you first when they want to hire a professional like you, or if they know of someone else who does. Just a few minutes of interaction per day can help you massively leverage LinkedIn to grow your professional business.

The disadvantage to organic marketing on LinkedIn is that it can take a fair amount of time to establish meaningful relationships with your audience and get found by them. If you are not regularly engaging at first, you may struggle to develop enough momentum to help your business grow enough on LinkedIn. You want to make sure that if you choose to grow on LinkedIn, that you regularly engage and that you spend time learning how to leverage this platform so that it can be functional and effective for your online business growth.

Paid LinkedIn Marketing

LinkedIn offers paid marketing features that enable you to increase your viewership and, as a result, increase your likelihood of getting discovered by your target audience. You can take advantage of LinkedIn's paid advertising features if you want to grow faster so that you can increase your momentum, get seen by your target audience faster, and maximize your conversions through this platform.

The biggest advantage to LinkedIn paid advertisements is that you can either manage the advertisements yourself or you can have LinkedIn professionals manage the advertisement for you so that you do not have to take care of the advertisement yourself. You can choose whichever option fits your needs, although you should note that having LinkedIn manage your advertisements will cost you more than managing it yourself as you will be paying not only for your advertisements but also for your professional management.

If you choose to use the self-serve option, you will need to decide what your ad format is going to be first. There are three types of ad formats you can choose from: sponsored content, text ads, or a hybrid that combines sponsored content and text ads. Sponsored content will appear in various places on LinkedIn no matter what device people are using to check their accounts on, and text ads are simple yet effective ads that will be displayed for members only.

Once you have chosen the format of your ad, you will need to create your ad by choosing what wording, images, and links (if any) you will include in your advertisement. Then, you will need to target your ad. You can target your ad by simply keying in your target audience in the campaign manager and selecting the options that highlight your target audience. LinkedIn will then tell you whether your audience is large enough or if it is just right so that you can maximize your visibility and engagement.

Lastly, you will need to set your budget. LinkedIn allows you to either pay per click or pay per impression, so you can choose the one that fits your needs the best. Then, all you need to do is set your budget for how much you want to spend for your advertisement so that LinkedIn knows how often to show your advertisement and to who. Then, if your budget runs out or your advertisement is getting seen by too expensive of an audience, LinkedIn can adjust your positioning to make sure that you are getting seen by the right people.

After you have chosen your audience and outlined your target audience, you can click "Confirm." LinkedIn will then determine whether or not your advertisement meets their community guidelines. As long as it does, they will approve your advertisement, and then all you will need to do is monitor the analytics relating to your advertisement to make sure that it is performing effectively. If not, you can make minor adjustments or pull the advertisement altogether and start fresh so that you can gain better results from your ads.

Chapter 10: Creating Your Strategy

Creating a social media strategy is simple, especially once you know what platforms you want to have your brand present on and how those platforms can be leveraged to grow your audience. Now that you have what you need to maximize your time on each platform, all you need to do is determine which platforms you are going to spend time on, how much time you are going to spend on them, and how you are going to leverage that time to get maximum visibility on the platform. The best way to do this is through the use of a content calendar and, if you desire, a "hub" that you can use to manage multiple social media accounts on from one place.

Content schedules are essentially schedules that are designed with the intention of recognizing at which times your account tends to get the most traction with its posts and then having you post at those times. So, say you get maximum leverage on your Instagram account at 9:00 AM on Tuesdays, you would schedule your daily Instagram post for 9:00 AM on Tuesdays. You could either create a post ahead of time and have it scheduled to release at that time, or you could set a reminder on your phone and simply log in and post at that time. How you choose to use the calendar, whether you want to use it to automate or simply to guide you, is up to you and how much time you are willing to spend posting and engaging each day. Your content calendar should account for posting times and engagement times on all platform that you will be spending time on online to make sure that you remain consistent and visible on all platforms.

Hubs or social media managers are applications like HootSuite or Buffer that allow you to post everything ahead of time on an application that will then release all your posts according to your schedule. These hubs can help with everything from responding to comments or messages to getting your content out there on a regular basis, which makes them powerful tools for people who are managing multiple platforms at once. You can pick the hub that provides you with the tools you need to manage all of your platforms so that you can grow effortlessly and in a balanced manner.

Conclusion

Congratulations on completing *Social Media Marketing Mastery!*

Social media can be intimidating or challenging if you are not familiar with it or if you have never used it for business before, but it does not have to be. Growing on social media can be an excellent opportunity for you to market to your audience across the globe, increase brand recognition, and get more sales flowing in through your business. Every single business model can thrive on social media no matter what your brand may be, which makes this a universally valuable tool for all.

I hope that by reading this book, you are able to begin feeling more comfortable with social media so that you can start mastering the process of building your own brand presence online. Through following this guide, you can now identify where you need to be spending your time online and how you can spend that time to maximize your growth. If you nail the process just right, it will be easy for you to continue growing so that you can continue scaling your business and increasing your bottom line.

The next step for you is to get on social media and start developing your presence. Get clear on what your objectives are and continue sharing on a consistent basis so that you can begin growing and developing momentum. Be sure to give yourself time to adapt to each platform, as there will be learning curves for you to embrace that will enable you to grow faster. Once you have embraced these learning curves and figured out the platforms, it will become easier for you to continually grow and increase your brand reach. As a result, you will have mastered your online presence and enabled your brand to grow faster than ever before.

If you need the added support, or if you prefer a streamlined organization, do not forget to check out hubs like HootSuite and Buffer. Sometimes, having that added support can be key in allowing you to grow faster by keeping everything together and simple. As well, they will support you in leveraging content calendars which are paramount in growing online through consistency and maximized visibility.

Lastly, if you enjoyed this book and felt that it supported you in learning how to master social media, I ask that you, please take the time to review it on Amazon Kindle. Your honest feedback would be greatly appreciated, as it supports me in creating even more high-quality content for you to enjoy.

Thank you, and best of luck in growing your online presence!

Insanely Effective Network and Multi-Level Marketing for Introverts on Social Media

Learn How to Build an MLM Business to Success by the Top Leaders in the Field and Why You NEED to Start RIGHT NOW!

By Ray Schreiter & Tom Higdon

Table of Contents

Creating Your Ad "Behind the Scenes"
Creating Your Ad "The Visual"
Confirming Your Ad
Boosted Posts

Chapter 5: Why Use Instagram?

Organic Instagram Advertising
Creating and Optimizing Your Instagram Profile
Designing Your Newsfeed
Hashtag Tips and Tricks
Engaging with Your Followers
Paid Instagram Marketing

Types of Instagram Advertisements

Chapter 6: Why Use Google?

Organic Google Advertising
SEO
Paid Google Advertising

Accessing Ad Manager
Creating Your Ad "Behind the Scenes"
Creating Your Ad "The Visual"

Chapter 7: Why Use Twitter?

Organic Twitter Advertising
Creating and Optimizing Your Twitter Profile
Getting Your Page Verified
Using Video Marketing on Twitter
Having A Post Schedule
Taking Advantage of Twitter Teams
Getting Involved in the Conversation
Posting Relevant Content
Paid Twitter Advertising

Introduction

Congratulations on downloading *Insanely Effective Network and Multi-Level Marketing for Introverts on Social Media*!

This book is the ultimate guide to help you understand how you can run a powerful network marketing or multi-level marketing business even if you are an introvert. Inside of these pages, you are going to learn everything you need to know to run a successful business that will earn you a great income and help you enjoy the life you truly aspire to live.

Network marketing companies and multi-level marketing (MLM) companies have had a highly controversial reputation in the past. Some people believe that they are incredible, and others believe that they are a scam. In this book, I am going to prove that they are not what people say they are and that you can definitely make a great amount of money through your network marketing company.

As soon as you learn these strategies and begin applying them into your business, you are going to discover that network marketing truly is not as hard as some people make it look. Furthermore, you do not have to resort to annoying and spammy marketing methods in order to make money with this business model. In fact, you do not want to be pushy or spammy at all. Instead, you want to focus on running a business that is going to have integrity and dignity. To do that, you may want to use what is known as "attraction marketing," which I will elaborate on in the succeeding chapters.

I am also going to show you how you can conduct a sales conversation, convert prospects into clients or distributors, and lead a team. Virtually everything you need to run a powerful network marketing business is outlined in this book. As long as you are willing to stay committed and put the work in, you can feel confident about generating the types of results that you want to create with your business.

If you want to get the maximum value out of this book, you need to be ready to put in the work. This book highlights the importance of knowing what to do and doing it properly. Everything you are going to learn is practical, effective, and guaranteed to help you attain the success you want in your MLM business.

It is important that you realize that in taking on this venture, you are taking personal responsibility for your business. You are responsible for your success and results, and it is up to you to put in the work needed to create them. If you want to experience massive success, you have to be dedicated to learning what it takes to generate massive success.

If you are ready to begin learning about how to have an incredible business that is going to help you generate maximum success and earn a great income, it's time to begin! Dive in to learn about what makes network marketing so great and how you can make work for you.

Chapter 1: What You Need to Know About Network Marketing and Multi-Level Marketing (MLM)

Network marketing and multi-level marketing (MLM) are two forms of businesses that are based on a peer-to-peer selling structure. Over the years, network marketing and MLM companies have gained a controversial reputation. Generally, those who take the time to learn how this structure works find themselves making a great deal of profit as opposed to those who don't. In fact, network marketing and MLM companies are known to have produced more millionaires than virtually any other industry to date.

There are many reasons why people join network marketing companies, but the biggest one is that it has the biggest potential to support you in reaching your income goals. Before I begin teaching you about how you can make a killing off of your network marketing business (even as an introvert), I want to show you what exactly you are getting into.

What Is the Difference Between Network Marketing and MLM?

Network marketing and MLM are both peer-to-peer selling structures, but they work in two unique ways. While network marketing is more based on direct sales, MLM focuses on building a team.

The network marketing structure is sometimes referred to as "direct sales" because the primary emphasis is on selling a product to consumers. Essentially, business is conducted through a middleman. The company that you are working for will sell you catalogues and other marketing materials, and then you go to your consumer and sell them the product. The consumer then purchases it, and the company compensates you for that sale.

In some cases, network marketing distributors choose to purchase some popular stocks to keep on hand so that they can get the product to the client faster. This increases appeal and supports the individual in generating more sales, but it is not necessary.

When it comes to starting a network marketing business, your primary focus is identifying potential customers in your network and selling them products. Because the market can be competitive, there are also many other ways to meet new people and add them to your list of prospects. I will show you exactly how to do that in this book!

MLM, on the other hand, is similar to network marketing, except that it involves including a team of distributors building underneath you. In network marketing, your primary focus was to sell products to potential customers. In MLM, however, you want to focus on selling to customers *and* recruiting other distributors. Based on the nature of the pay scale, you are encouraged to invite other people to become distributors underneath you. In doing so, you build what is called a team or a downline.

With MLM, you are paid in more ways than just selling to customers. You are also paid for your downline and everything they sell, too. So, in this case, you stand to make a lot more money if you are willing to put in the effort to have people join underneath you. In this book, I will also cover how you can build a team and how you can be a strong leader so that your team earns more money and, as a result, so do you.

Should I Start Network Marketing or Build My Own Business from Scratch?

Before you launch into any new business venture, you always want to make sure that you are making the right choice. In this case, you might be wondering if you should go with network marketing or MLM, or if you should just build your own business from scratch. While you are certainly welcome to do anything you desire, I want to make sure that you understand exactly what comes with either option.

When you choose to start a business from scratch, you are choosing to take on a lot of work. For people who know exactly what they want to do or are passionate about making products or services to sell, this can be a great option. However, they must also realize that this comes with a lot more responsibility, too. Launching your own business means that you are solely responsible for things, such as branding, marketing, creating products or services, selling, incorporating, handling legal fees and taxes, managing your online presence, and more. Depending on the nature of the company, you might have to work on supplier acquisition and finding stockists who will actually sell your products. Then, to top it off, you also have to shoulder all of the financial aspects related to starting the business. You could always consider a loan, but then you have to pay that money back plus interest. If you were to choose investors, you would have to factor in their thoughts and opinions, which could get messy.

On the other hand, network marketing and MLM are a lot simpler. You can still choose an industry and products or services that you are passionate about. Then, all you have to do is market the products to prospective clients. You are not responsible for finding and hiring manufacturers, storing products, shipping products to clients, managing websites, and the like. You simply purchase your marketing materials, market the products, and receive your commission for doing so. However, because you are an independent distributor, you are still classified as an entrepreneur, and you carry all of the great benefits of being one, i.e. setting your own schedule and having an unlimited earning potential.

What Benefits Do I Gain from Network Marketing Companies?

There are several benefits that you can gain from working with a network marketing or MLM company. Aside from setting your own schedule and having an unlimited earning potential, there are many other reasons why people love getting involved in these companies.

One major reason is that when you join a network marketing company, there is a smaller amount of risk that you incur. With your own company, you put a lot of your own money and assets on the line to start the business. When you are a distributor with an MLM company, however, the company itself takes on any liability. This means that if anyone has any complaints, money is lost, or time is wasted, it is lost by the company and not you. You still receive your check, either way, as long as you have sold your products and services.

Another benefit you stand to gain is that you are marketing products that are already tested and known for high quality. When you are starting your own business, testing products and finding high-quality ones can be costly and time-consuming. When you start with an MLM company, this process has already been done. Anytime a new product comes to the product line for you to market, it has already undergone testing and experiments to make sure that it is high quality. As a result, you can always be confident in the quality of the products that you are marketing to your audience.

When you choose to go with a network marketing or MLM company, you have the unique opportunity of generating what is known as a "residual income." Residual income is, essentially, income that you gain but do not have to trade a direct amount of hours in exchange for a set amount of money. In other words, once you have your downline established and customers who are regularly purchasing products, your money will continue coming in. While you will still want to focus on growth, a certain amount of your income will already be practically guaranteed every month. This means that you can focus on spending time doing things that you love rather than trading your time for a paycheck.

If you are the type of person who loves the idea of a freedom-based lifestyle where you can do anything you want, go anywhere you want, and do it all whenever you want, MLM and network marketing are a wonderful solution for you. These companies are generally based online in the modern world—meaning you can do virtually anything you want and go anywhere you want without worrying about your business. Instead, you can easily take trips, go on vacations, move around, or live the nomad lifestyle all while making more cash.

There are clearly many reasons why network marketing is a powerful business model when done right. As long as you follow the strategies I give you in this book, there is no reason why you cannot be another one of the millionaires earning their income through independent sales.

Chapter 2: Master Your Mindset Above All Else

Before you can achieve anything, you need to focus on mastering the mindset associated with the success of your venture. When it comes to a business venture like network marketing or MLM sales, you are going to find that there are many people with many different opinions. Sometimes, those opinions are not optimistic. In fact, some of them can be the exact opposite. If you do not spend time getting crystal clear with your own mindset and energy, you are going to find yourself struggling to stay optimistic in your business. If you have a hard time staying optimistic and excited, your customers and team will struggle, too. Then, your business will most likely fail.

I suggest starting with mindset first because it can ensure that you are mentally prepared for any challenges that you may face starting from day one. This does not mean that it will be a challenge right off the bat, but as with anything, there will be a learning curve. Ensuring that you are mentally prepared to withstand this learning curve and generate success will keep you on track to earn a great deal of money in your business in the long run.

The strategies that I am going to give you in this chapter are ones that you need to start exercising right away. Some of these strategies are going to be ones that you need to be doing on a daily basis. Others are ones that you can reserve for when you are having a hard time in your business and need an extra boost of optimism to keep you going. Having these in your toolkit now and practicing them from day one will strengthen the impact that these tools have on you. As a result, they will work exactly as you need them to when it comes to helping you achieve the success that you desire from your business.

Envision Your Dreamy End Goal

The first thing you need to do before starting your MLM business is to dream about what you want it all to look like. Spend some time really engaging in the dream and deciding everything that you want to have. In order to do this productively and effectively, make sure that you are dreaming as if there are no limitations on what you can do, as there really aren't any. If money, time, and resources were not an issue, what exactly would you want to be doing with your business—with your life? Get deep and insightful with this vision, and be as specific as you can.

If you want, you can create a vision board for this. Find pictures, words, articles, and anything else you desire that reflects what is in your dream. Then, keep the vision board handy so that you can see it at least once per day. This is a wonderful way to motivate yourself and stay focused.

Spend 10 Minutes A Day Dreaming

As you work on building your business, commit to spending 10 minutes every single day to dreaming. Spend this time dreaming about what you want the end result to be like, what it will feel like, and how you are going to enjoy it. You can do this in any way you want. You might spend that ten minutes dreaming about what the perfect day would look like, looking at a highlight reel of all of your best achievements, or simply enjoying the dream of doing one thing that you long to do when you achieve your success.

Research suggests that spending just ten minutes every day dreaming about your desires supports you in manifesting them. During this ten minutes, you mentally prepare yourself for the lifestyle and demands that will be placed upon you from having the success that you desire. This is a great way to overcome feelings of worthlessness, to prepare yourself for the changes, and to mentally understand what will be required in order for you to get there. When you imagine yourself doing it, the process of actually getting there and believing that it is possible is not so hard.

List 3 Things You Want to Achieve and Achieve Them

Every single day, you can work toward conditioning yourself for success and discipline by setting a goal to accomplish three things. Then, make sure that you actually accomplish them. These three things should, in one way or another, be tied in with your success, even if they include taking a nap so that you can be more rested for running your business.

By setting small goals daily, you set yourself up for success by conditioning your mind to want to achieve your goals. Each time you achieve these smaller goals, your mind feels a rush of endorphins like serotonin that reward it for the accomplishment. As a result, you become far more excited by success, and it is easier for you to continue working toward larger goals. Plus, these smaller goals are the necessary steps toward actually reaching your larger goals. It is a win-win situation!

Give Yourself a Pep Talk

During times that you are struggling in your business, refrain from bullying yourself or getting caught up in self-doubt and pessimism. It can be easy to feel as though ruts are forever or somehow permanent, but they're not. Each time you find yourself feeling as though you are in a rut or noticing the energy of self-doubt creeping in, set the intention to give yourself a pep talk. As soon as you notice it, start.

Pep talks do not have to be hard or elaborate. Simply reminding yourself of your dream and reminding yourself that you have what it takes is enough. You might consider recalling times that you faced adversity and overcame it with strength and success, or even reminding yourself as to the many reasons why you wanted to start your business in the first place. Staying focused on the end goal is the best way to continue giving yourself pep talks as needed so that you can experience greater success in your business. Pep talks can be a part of your daily routine, or they can be reserved for those moments when you are feeling as though the route to success is more of a struggle than you had anticipated it would be.

Hold Yourself Accountable

When it comes to generating success on any level, you have to be willing to hold yourself accountable. When you make a commitment, be the kind of person who is willing to do whatever it takes to see that commitment come through. It can be challenging at times, but it is essential. Not only will fulfilling the commitment bring you one step closer to achieving success, but it will also help you prove to yourself that you are capable of doing so.

Anytime you make a commitment to do something—whether it is to yourself, to your downline, or to your customers—be impeccable with your word. Do not go back on your commitment, and do not hold back from achieving success. Make sure you do everything you can to stay true to your word. If, for some reason, you absolutely cannot, make sure that you come up with a viable solution or alternative to help you, your downline or your customer achieve their goals. Your commitment and your devotion are necessary: no one else is going to do this for you. Start from day one, and you will be mentally dressed for success.

Pay Attention to Your Thoughts

Your thoughts have the capacity to build you up or tear you down. They can do the same for your business, too. If you are not staying disciplined with your thoughts, you might find yourself mentally sabotaging your success. You need to trust that you have what it takes to succeed and consciously dim down the inner voice that keeps telling you that you can't. Anytime you notice it coming up and telling you that you are incapable, unworthy, or unable to succeed, begin affirming to yourself that you are capable, worthy, and able of creating success.

Be willing to notice these thoughts and take control. Consciously choose to think thoughts that are going to help move you toward success, rather than take you away from it. When you put the effort into thinking positive thoughts, your ability to stay optimistic is significantly improved. This means that it will be easier for you to stay focused and generate the success you want because your own inner pessimism will not be sabotaging your results.

Build an Inspiring Team of People

Sometimes, nothing is more helpful than an empowering and inspiring system of support helping you succeed. In MLM businesses, you have a unique opportunity to build a team of people who are all working toward the same goals on one level or another. As a result, you can selectively choose to build your team in a way that supports success right from the very beginning.

When you are building your team of downlines, focus on using the advice I give you in this book to develop a strong community of people. Through this, you can create a culture of positivity, optimism, support, and inspiration. As a result, all of you will have a powerful team to fall back on any time you are feeling discouraged or doubtful with your business. This support network is unparalleled in how it will help you and your entire team continually work toward success.

Stay Curious

The power of curiosity is magnificent. When you are curious, you search for answers. You can use this curiosity as a way to magnify success in your business and keep you moving forward. Stay curious about what lies in store for you. Stay curious about where a little bit more effort or the next level can do for you. Stay curious about what you can achieve. Stay curious about everything. The more curious you are, the more wonders you will be filled with. This energy keeps you looking and moving forward.

Replace your fear with curiosity. Replace your doubt with curiosity. Replace your discouragement with curiosity. Replace anything holding you back mentally with a sense of curiosity. Wonder what you can do, and then seek to find the answers by moving forward and staying committed and focused. When you do this, success becomes much easier because you are curious about just how much you can achieve, rather than worried that you may not achieve any at all.

Chapter 3: Choosing The Right Company for You

Now that you are equipped with a powerful mindset that is ready to succeed, it is time to equip yourself with a company that can get you there! Choosing the right company is essential. Once you choose your company, you need to stay committed. This is how you are going to maintain your branding, keep your image intact, become known as the "go-to" person for that product or service, and climb the ranks. Each time you restart with a new company, you have to rebrand yourself, get the word out there, and rebuild your downline. Rather than having to put in the work multiple times, it is better just to commit and do it all once! To be able to do so requires that you have the right company to support you along the way.

In this chapter, I am going to show you exactly what you need to consider and how you can find the right company for you. You are going to discover what matters, what is required in order for you to achieve success in your business, and how you can discover if a company is going to be a perfect fit for your long-term when it comes to achieving your goals. I must stress the importance of making sure that the company you desire to join fits *all* of the criteria. Do not join a company just because your good friend did, or you might end up with a company that will not serve you long-term. Look at the following criteria, and think critically before starting. Remember: this is a business move, and it needs to be treated like one.

Choose Your Niche and Discover Companies

Before you can evaluate a company for whether or not it is worth your time, you need to consider what companies you want to evaluate! This requires you to identify what niche you want to be a part of and what companies exist within that niche. There are a few ways that you can do this, but ultimately, it comes with finding a niche that you are passionate about, that is profitable, and that has a strong MLM company in it that you can join. Without these three factors, the company might not be worth your while.

To determine what niche you want to be in, consider your top two or three interests that you feel could be profitable. There are many out there, such as health and beauty, fashion, finances, career, and more. Consider what ones are the most interesting and important to you and start there.

After you have determined which your top two or three are, I want you to evaluate them in terms of how profitable they are going to be. You need to pick a niche that is going to have the capacity to earn you a great deal of money. If you pick one that is too small or not growing, you will quickly realize how hard it is and that you may not actually be able to make a profit in that niche. You want to do some online research to discover the size of the niche, who the target audience is, how much money it earns, and whether or not it is growing. If it is growing and has a strong audience size, chances are it is a great place for you to get into.

Lastly, do another search to find out which companies are in your desired niche. This shouldn't be too hard; simply type in "(chosen niche) MLM companies in (your country)." This will bring up a list of all of the different niches available to you in your country that fall under your niche. I suggest writing all of these names down and doing research on all of them to make sure that you don't overlook a potentially great candidate.

Consider the Stability and Longevity of the Company

When you are looking into the companies that you have identified, there are some critical pieces of information that you need to pay attention to. In particular, you need to focus on determining how strong the company is, how stable it is, and how long it is likely to be in business for. Some companies are in business for decades and continue to grow with great strength. Others die off after only a couple of years. It is important that you pick one that is going to last and stay stable so that you can continue making an income for a long time.

It is important that you realize that if the company does go under, you will lose everything with them. You want to pick one that is going to stay around for a long time and that will continue giving you the opportunity to earn a greater income. You can learn about this through a few different points of information.

The first thing that you need to consider is how well-capitalized the company is. You want one that has plenty of capital to grow, that is continuing to focus on growth by launching new products and services or opportunities, and that has a clean track record for paying people their commissions. One that seems to have very little extra capital or that struggles to grow or pay its distributors is one that you should avoid, as these are companies that are beginning to show signs of potential failure.

Another thing that you need to consider is how old the company is. Companies that are less than five years do offer ground-floor opportunities and, if you have a good eye for such things, could be a great opportunity. After all, if you are one of the earliest distributors, you are more likely to grow people under you. However, if you are a ground-floor distributor on a company that does not succeed, this doesn't mean much. If you are not entirely sure about how to evaluate the longevity of a business *idea,* which is an entirely different book altogether, you are better off choosing a company that has been around for at least five years. This shows that the company is out of the startup phase and has reached a degree of stability that should keep it around for many years to come.

Evaluate the Products and Services

In addition to evaluating the company itself, you need to evaluate the products that they are selling, too. You want to make sure that you are choosing to sell for a company that has unique products. If their products are too similar to something that you can buy in store or elsewhere, chances are your audience will flock to that option instead because it's simply easier and faster than waiting for the shipment to come in. However, if your product is unique, your audience will understand why it is worth the wait and will have nowhere else to go to avoid shipping times.

You also have to make sure that the products being sold by the company are desirable. The last thing you want to do is find yourself trying to sell products that people truly do not want. Your product needs to provide tremendous value to the customer if it is going to be able to sell, so pay attention to this. In addition, make sure that your unique and desirable product is priced right. The last thing you want to do is find yourself trying to market something that is priced higher than the average customer is willing to spend. The only people who will purchase things at these higher prices are other distributors so that they can reach their compensation plan goals, which can put you in a difficult position when it comes to selling products and growing your business.

Lastly, make sure that the product you are choosing is not just the result of a trend or a fad. Choosing something that is likely to be irrelevant or obsolete in a few months' or years' time can result in you putting a lot of work into building your business only for it to fall flat when people move on to the next trend. While businesses that incorporate trends into their products to maximize sales are genius, businesses who build their entire company based off of a trend are not. The former knows how to expertly use trends to boost sales, whereas the latter does not have a strong plan for future growth, meaning that there likely won't be any. You do not want to be stuck with your wheels spinning on a business that loses its marketability in a few months or years. Instead, you want one with products that will continue to serve your audience for a long time to come.

Learn About the Compensation Plan

Since you are getting into this business to get paid, it is essential that you pay attention to the compensation plan. Choosing a company with a poor compensation plan is going to result in you struggling to earn a strong enough profit. In fact, you may even find yourself earning virtually nothing at all. There is nothing more tragic than hearing stories of people who have put tons of effort and attention into their businesses and climbed the rankings only to be several levels up in the company and still earning just a couple hundred bucks a month.

You need to choose a company that is going to help you start earning a lot as soon as possible. This comes from picking a company that has a great compensation plan. There is no fixed framework for what constitutes a great compensation plan. As long as you don't find yourself putting in tons of work and being paid pennies for it, the plan should be considered a good one. However, as you go about comparing companies to determine which ones are the best, you should compare compensation plans, too. That way, you can choose the company with the best plan that meets the other criteria and fits your needs.

Also, pay attention to bonuses. Most companies offer bonuses if you hit certain goals or if you achieve certain achievements. While these do not necessarily have to be the deciding factor for you, knowing what you can expect to earn on top of your regular commissions can be nice. Choosing companies that love to offer bonuses regularly and that offer many other prizes or rewards for reaching certain targets can be nice. Typically, these companies are more considerate of their distributors and will offer better incentives to work your business. This can mean plenty of wonderful bonuses and added benefits for doing the same amount of work!

Pay Attention to The Specific Team You're Joining

Aside from the company itself, pay attention to the team that you are considering joining under. The company and products are both essential to your success, but so is a strong team. Starting a new network marketing company without a strong team can result in you not having the inspiration, motivation, and support when you need it. Alternatively, it can result in you feeling outcast if the team is too cliquey and does not make room for new team members. Unfortunately, this can happen, and it can be a big discouragement when it comes to running your business.

Ideally, your team and the person introducing you to the opportunity should be committed to helping you succeed. You should feel confident that they are going to be just as committed before you join as they will be after, too. Finding a team that is filled with strong leaders who are committed to helping each other succeed ensures that you are going to have all of the resources that you need to succeed. In addition, it will show you how you can best lead your own team so that you can stay committed to their success, too.

A good way to discover more about your potential team is to ask about who the team is, how it is led, what types of activities are involved, and what the support is like. You want a team and a leader who are going to train you for success, not just ones who are going to recruit you, collect a check, and abandon you to move on to their next recruit. If your sponsor will let you, consider asking for a chance to take a "sneak peek" at what the team is like by inviting you to a training call or event. This is a great way to get an inside-view at how the team works together and if they will be able to support you and your future team in creating success going forward.

Determine If the Business Fits with Your Goals

Remember the dream you dreamed up in the last chapter? Here is a great way for you to begin calling upon that dream to start serving you right now. Consider that dream, and consider each business and how it would fit into your dream. Does it have the offers that you want? Is the opportunity the right fit? Does it make sense? If you find a company that serves you with everything you need to make your dream come true, chances are you have found a great company.

You always want to make sure that your MLM company fits into your life, not the other way around. You should not feel like you are trying to adjust your life to fit the needs of the business. After all, this is what you are likely trying to get away from when leaving your job. Learning how to fit your business into your life properly can take time and practice, as you have to learn how to let go of your employee mentality and let your company factor you in, not the other way around. However, once you learn how to view your opportunity from the eyes of a boss, it becomes a lot easier to see how the company is going to fit into your lifestyle and support you in creating your dream life.

If the company does not have the potential to fulfill your dream life alongside you, chances are it may not be the right one for you. Even if it is a great company with great earning potential and profitability, you do not want to pick a company at the expense of your happiness. You need something that you can be passionate about and that will bring you joy. Believe me—if you pick a company that you are not passionate about, people are going to be able to tell, and growing your company will be a lot more challenging. Your passion is infectious, so you are likely to grow much faster with a company you are genuinely passionate about than one that you are not, even if the opportunity seems better on paper.

Making The Final Pick of Which Company You Choose

Once you have put all of your consideration in towards your choice, it is time to choose! Choosing at this point should be simple, but I want to make sure that you feel confident in making your choice. So, to recap: you want a company that will be around for a long time with great products that customers want and are willing to pay for. You also want to make sure that their compensation plan is strong enough to earn you a great profit, that it will help you grow quickly, and that it will not take too long or be too challenging to begin earning that profit. The team you are considering to join needs to be inspiring and supportive and willing to train you so that you can achieve your desired success. You also need to have a genuine passion for the company and products that you will be selling, as you do not want to find yourself in a company that you do not enjoy. If you are unsure about whether or not you are passionate about the company and their products, consider starting out as a customer first. Then, if you do feel that you are passionate enough to sell them, you can consider them as a potential business opportunity.

If your ideal business meets all of the above criteria, chances are it is a great business to start with. This is everything you need to create a strong opportunity to build a massive business that is going to help you get rich and earn residual income, so it is essential that you are a stickler about having these criteria met. If even one of these areas is weak, you might risk your ability to earn enough money to make your dreams come true. It absolutely must be the right fit for you if you are going to succeed.

Chapter 4: Making A Commitment to Growth

If you want to have a successful business, you need to have growth. A business without growth is just a failure. You do not want your business to fail, so you need to commit to growth. This is how you are going to ensure that your business succeeds and that you earn the income that you desire through your business.

When it comes to committing to growth in favor of your business, there are two areas that you need to commit to—personal growth and professional growth. Both of these areas of growth are going to support you in achieving the magnitude of growth required to experience success.

Personal growth is going to support you in growing in a way that supports your success. Personal growth contributes to your ability to mentally handle the growth that you are facing, to see the good in everything, and to stay positive and in an optimal state of mind to achieve your growth. If you let yourself stop growing, it will be a challenge to grow your business because you will not have the commitment or drive that you need to continue climbing the rankings to success.

Professional growth is important, as this is going to teach you how you can do better at your business. You want to know how you can become a better leader, a better seller, and a better marketer. You want to pay attention to opportunities to discover how you can learn more about your product and industry so that you become a great resource for your downline and customers. Also, you want to make sure that you can understand what it takes to grow and put in the work required to do so.

When you commit to your personal and professional growth and put an honest effort into both, achieving success becomes inevitable. That is because you are ensuring that you have all of the resources and knowledge required to make success happen. I have outlined below how you can begin achieving personal and professional growth right now so that you can grow your business to be a beautiful empire right off the bat.

Learn to See the Good in Things

Learning how to see the good in everything is a wonderful way to begin discovering opportunities everywhere. Realistically, everything is an opportunity for growth or success. All you need to do is know how to see the opportunity and take advantage of it to put it to work for you. If you want to achieve growth and excellence, you need to learn how you can see the good in things around you so that your eyes stay open and that your mind stays optimistic.

In addition to helping you see opportunities that you can take advantage of, learning to see the good in things is going to help you train your downline to do the same. As a result, you will end up having a strong team of individuals who are committed to growth and excellence, too. This will support all of you in seeing opportunities and continually working toward growth so that each of you continues to experience great success in their businesses.

Commit to Working Hard Toward Success

Hard work pays off. While your business will not always be hard, staying committed and focused is essential, and being willing to put in the work is the only way to achieve success. When you are working, focus on spending the least amount of time doing the most productive tasks possible. This will ensure that your time is spent working hard and achieving results that translate to growth. It will also keep you from wasting any time or spinning your wheels trying to achieve more growth while doing things that are not really getting you anywhere. The people who have the most time are the ones who use theirs wisely.

Hard work does not necessarily require you to be doing back-breaking labor or putting yourself through the ringer every single day just to see growth. Instead, focus on doing things that push you out of your comfort zone and force you to take the next steps toward the next level. Put effort into getting out of your head and into your plan so that you can take the necessary action to create the growth that you desire. Then, do it again. Keep doing it until you achieve success.

Continue Approaching Growth with Consistency and Passion

The more you stay consistent and passionate about what you are doing, the easier it is going to be for you to continue growing. Without consistency, your passion has nowhere to be applied. Without passion, your consistent effort lacks soul and purpose. You want to keep everything focused and working toward your goals with a strong level of passion and drive.

Consistency and passion are going to do two things for your business: they will keep you in the right frame of mind to grow, and they will keep your audience paying attention to you. Because you are setting the pace for yourself, continuing to put in the effort required to achieve success is a lot easier. You become used to it, and your commitment to growing your business becomes an enjoyable routine that you look forward to every single day.

In addition, because your audience sees you staying passionate and continually talking about your opportunity and products, they become curious. When people realize that you are serious about what you are doing and that you are committed to making growth happen in your business, they focus on you more. They realize that there is probably a reason as to why you are still passionate about your business, and they grow curious about what it is and why you have not given up yet. Hence, they are more likely to want to try it out. If you stay committed and passionate, your team and customers will, too.

Respect Yourself and Your Needs

When it comes to growth, committing to understanding yourself better and having a greater sense of self-awareness is important. Understanding yourself and your needs and respecting yourself enough to advocate for yourself ensures that you always feel as though you are working in satisfying or desirable conditions. This ensures that you are never feeling overworked, taken advantage of, or mistreated in your company or business.

People who do not advocate for themselves and practice self-respect for their needs find themselves feeling rundown and exhausted. As a result, their businesses suffer. They may not have the energy to keep up anymore, or they may even find themselves resenting their businesses and avoiding doing them. Since you own your business and you are the only person holding yourself accountable, if you let yourself feel rundown to the point where you do not want to work anymore, no one can stop you. As a result, you might end up giving up on the very business that could have brought you the success that you desire.

Rather than letting yourself get run down and resentful, pay attention to your needs, and make sure that they get fulfilled. If you feel that you have been working hard and that you need a break, schedule some time off. If you feel that you are giving a great deal to your team and not enough to yourself, let them know that you are taking some time off, or consider asking some of your more knowledgeable distributors to begin supporting you in training new team members. As you grow and as your needs change, always make sure that you are taking account for them and respecting yourself in the process. The more you take care of yourself and feel good about doing your business, the easier it is going to be for you to generate growth in your company.

Focus On Expanding in Every Way That You Can

A commitment to growth means a commitment to expansion. You need to be committed to expanding in every way possible: from learning more about yourself and how you work best to discovering more about your company and how you can grow even bigger. The more you commit to expansion, the easier it is going to be for you to identify opportunities and grow. Then, once you see these opportunities, make sure that you also make a commitment to actually giving them a try.

While you may not want to put work into every single opportunity, and while you might find out that they will not bring you as much benefit as you have hoped along the way, the effort you put in will teach you a lot. As you learn to identify these opportunities, you will teach yourself to discover which ones are worth following and which ones might not be the best idea. Then, you can begin following the ones that are worth your while and applying all of your knowledge and skill into making them a success.

The more you recognize unique opportunities and commit to giving everything a try and learning as much as you can, the more you stand to learn. When the business owner becomes complacent and believes that they have already learned everything that they need to know, this is when they begin to lose out. This is especially true for business owners who rely on marketing as their primary source of income. Marketing is constantly changing, so committing to knowing more and doing more is the best way to ensure that you are going to learn everything you need to know to master the expansion in your industry.

Be Willing to Seek and Accept Feedback from Others

We can only see so much in the mirror and in our self-awareness and self-reflection. As humans, we simply cannot pick up on everything that we do and criticize it so that we can discover how to do better. While we can certainly learn a great deal, there will be things that we miss over or that we may not even realize that required growth or development.

Asking for feedback from those who work with you on a regular basis and taking it critically is a great way to begin discovering ways that you can grow more. When you spend time listening to what other people notice and giving them the opportunity to guide you, it allows you to have a spotlight shone on areas of yourself that you may not see otherwise. Feedback is a wonderful way to recognize new opportunities for how you can grow and do better in your life and in your business.

When you are listening to feedback, always make a conscious effort to refrain from getting judgmental or defensive when people offer it. It can be difficult to take feedback in a constructive way that supports you in actually learning more and doing better with what you learn. However, once you discover how much you can learn by listening and taking in the feedback that you are given, you will find that you can grow so much more when you are open-minded. Listen carefully to what people say, and think about it critically before discovering ways that you can apply the information to your growth. That way, you ensure that every adjustment you make and all the growth you work toward is actually supporting you in moving in the direction that you desire to go.

Lastly, when it comes to receiving feedback, always be cautious about who your feedback is coming from. While most feedback is well-meaning, you do not want to be taking too much feedback from people who do not understand your goals or who are unaware of what it takes to do what you desire to do. Taking feedback from people who are not actively educated on what it takes to do what you want to do might end up in you growing in the wrong direction or wasting your time on growth that is ineffective. Instead, try paying attention to those who you look up to and focus on learning more from them. These are the people who understand what you are doing more clearly and can offer you feedback that will actually help move you in the direction you want to go.

Commit to Learning About Your Business and Industry

No matter how long you are in your industry or business, you can guarantee that things are going to change. The more you commit to learning about your industry and staying educated on your business, the easier it is going to be for you to become a powerful resource to your downline and customers. Committing to becoming a knowledgeable resource means that people can count on you and come to you for advice and support when needed.

When people begin realizing that you know everything that they could possibly need to know about your business or industry, they begin to see you as an expert. Being seen as the expert means that people are going to trust that you are the one to go to when they need support. They will also point their friends and family in your direction because they know that you will have the answers they need. This results in greater exposure for yourself and your business—meaning a greater number of opportunities for growth and increased sales and recruitment volumes. It is well worth it to continue studying your business and industry so that you can become the expert and people come to you rather than searching for a different resource to help them.

Chapter 5: Promoting Your Products and Events

Having products and events where sales are involved is only worthwhile if you are actually going to promote them! As a network marketer or MLM distributor, your primary job is to promote your products and services and any events that you may have going on. This way, people know about you and what you are currently selling or where they can find you to get more products.

When it comes to MLM and network marketing it is essential that you promote effectively. Unfortunately, some people have a negative idea of what distributors are and how they market as a result of a few people in the industry who have had little to no training. However, you are going to learn how to market effectively, respectfully, with integrity, and in a way that actually *works.* In this chapter, I am going to show you the best updated strategies that are going to help you earn more customers and distributors using what is known as attraction marketing.

Build A Brand for Yourself

As a direct marketer, you are not bound to only the brand that is established by the company you are marketing for. In fact, if you want to be known as memorable and encourage people to purchase from you and not a different distributor, you do not want to focus solely on that brand at all. Instead, you want to focus on building a personal brand for yourself. Remember when I said that you want your business to fit into your life, not the other way around? This is a great opportunity to prove that this is the case.

When it comes to personal branding, you want to show your audience your entire lifestyle and how your company fits into it. This is going to achieve two things that support your business's growth. First, it will show your audience that you are a real person. People do not want to buy from someone who's entire page looks like an online catalogue. Instead, they want to buy from someone who has a personality and spends time bonding with their audience and building relationships with them. This has more meaning and feels better to your customer, helping them feel more interested in purchasing from you and feeling like they are personally appreciated for doing so.

Second, building a brand for yourself and showing off how your business fits into your life is a great way to show your audience how it could work for them, too. People who might be interested in starting a similar business will get to see how much fun you have and how the business becomes a part of your life. Because they also live a life, they will be able to relate to the life you are living. This allows them to begin thinking about how the company could potentially fit into their own life, too. As a result, half of the work is already done in getting them to join your team! All you have to do is give them the extra words of encouragement, and before you know it, you will have new members joining your team in no time.

Take Advantage of Video Marketing

Video marketing is growing in popularity. Even though you might be fearful of doing video marketing if you are an introvert, learning to master video marketing is a great way to start promoting your products and events. People love seeing and interacting with people on video because it feels real and personal. If you are worried about doing videos on your own, you might consider inviting a fellow distributor or a friend who is also a customer on video with you as you chat about new products. Doing this once or twice might be a great way to help you warm up to the idea of being on camera without feeling like all of the spotlight is on you.

Another way to grow used to video marketing is to start by just using stories. Facebook and Instagram story features allow you to upload 10-second video clips of you talking about a product, showing off a new product, or showing your excitement for the product that you are using. Also, they are not live so you can redo the film as many times as you desire before hitting "send."

If you want to begin moving into live videos and video marketing but are worried about doing so, starting a Facebook group and inviting your friends and family to join is a great way to begin. There, you can do videos just in front of those who you already feel comfortable in front of. Then, as this becomes more comfortable for you, you can begin moving into doing it on your personal page or your Facebook business page.

Create Content Specifically for Your Ideal Client

Since most businesses are conducted online these days, learning how to market directly to your ideal client is important. The online marketplace is massive, so marketing to the right client is essential. There is a saying in the marketing world that goes, "If you are not specific about who you are talking to, then you are talking to no one." This is completely true. Knowing how to market to the specific demographic that you want to sell to is imperative if you are going to successfully reach and attract new prospects who are actually interested in what you are selling.

Creating ideal content comes from knowing who your demographic is. Since you are already with a network marketing company or an MLM company, all you need to do is perform a quick web search to discover who the company's general demographic is. If the demographic is broad, such as "women in their 30s," focus on choosing a more specific niche for yourself. For example, say you are selling a healthy coffee that can support them in having greater energy and burning more fat. You might consider targeting "mothers in their 30s" or "busy businesswomen in their 30s." Picking a more specific audience will ensure that you are marketing to a specific person. This is how you are going to be able to pick and write relatable content, appeal to your audience better, and attract prospects. If you try marketing to the entire demographic, you are going to end up sounding confused and attempting to appeal to far too many people with completely different reasons as to why they might be interested in your product. Rather than helping you attract a larger audience, this will simply confuse your potential audience and drive them away to someone who is being more specific and intentional about their target prospect.

Once you know who you are talking to, you can begin creating content that caters specifically to those individuals. To do so, you want to focus on two things: speaking with the same type of language that they speak with and referencing the same types of experiences that they are likely to have. When you speak in a way that your audience can relate to, they are far more likely to pay attention to you and listen to what you have to say. Then, all you need to do is share regularly.

Make sure that as you share, you share a variety of things. Many of your posts should be focused solely on creating connections and showing people into your life. Remember: you want to give people the opportunity to learn about who you are, how they can relate to you, and how your products or business opportunity may fit into their lifestyle. This is how you are going to come across as human and interactive and build relationships so that people are more interested in and attracted to your opportunity.

Attend Events That Your Audience Would Attend

When it comes to bringing your products or services to events, always make sure that you are attending events that are actually relevant to what your audience would attend. Even though an event may be a great price, attending one that does not have the right audience could result in you wasting time and money. Furthermore, attending an event and having a poor turnout can feel like a blow to your self-esteem and lead to sensations of self-doubt. Instead of wasting your time and money and setting yourself up to feel bad, make sure that the only events you attend are ones that are relevant to your audience.

The same goes for online events: do not host events that your ideal audience is not likely to join. At one time in online MLM businesses, simply creating an event on Facebook and inviting a bunch of friends was enough to create a party that would earn you money. These days, doing that can result in your audience feeling annoyed because they may feel that too many people are doing this on a consistent basis. This can result in them completely ignoring you because they are tired of receiving these unsolicited invites. Instead, focus on creating a fun event and market for it. Do not invite people unless they have asked to be invited; or you have approached them, and they have agreed. This ensures that everyone joining wants to be there and is already a prospective client or recruit. In addition, this proves that you are not like other marketers and that you value people's freedom of choice. Because of this, people who say no now may say yes in the future because they do not need to worry that you will spam them with offers and sales pitches.

Show the Products in Use

Sharing pictures of your products or sales is an ineffective way to actually market to your audience. Remember: people have been doing this for a long time, and most people are annoyed with this behavior. In most cases, instead of earning you a sale, it will lose you some friends or followers online. Instead of being the person that people avoid, focus on creating an attraction marketing plan. This means that instead of sharing static pictures of a product or sales advertisements that your company created on your wall, share pictures of you actively using the products.

Anytime you receive a new shipment of products, take a few moments to hop on a video or into your stories and begin talking about the products and how they work. Do not just show pictures of the products or hold them up and talk in monotone. Instead, show how the products work. Do not be afraid to create live tutorials, sneak-peeks, and other types of content that allow you to show off how the products work in use. This is a great way to help your audience get a real insight as to what the products actually are, how they work, and why they are awesome.

You do not have to rely solely on video to share the products, either. Putting the product to work and then taking a picture and captioning about what the product is, why you love it, and how it works are also great ways to share the product in use. You can also invite your clients to share pictures or videos of them using the product as well. This can be a great way to show that you are not the only one in love with them but that those who are purchasing the products from you are, too.

As you show the products in use, rather than trying to end your show off in a hard sales pitch, simply invite people to message you if they are interested in knowing more about the product. This is a gentler way of inviting people in and is generally received better by those who you are marketing to. Creating hard sales pitches at the end of enjoyable posts can minimize the quality of them by making people instantly tune out and move on. People love to hear about how great the products that you are promoting are and how much you are loving them, but they want to feel like the idea to message you was their own and not pressured on them by you. When it comes to attraction-based marketing, the less pressure you apply, the better. Instead, show them why they need to make the choice to message you by showing off how great the products are and how much they're changing yours and your client's lives!

Don't Focus Entirely on Sales

As I mentioned above, the more you put pressure on people the more you are going to pressure them into unfollowing you or unfriending you. People are always happy to shop or learn more, but they want to feel like it was their own decision to do so. Creating regular sales pitches and constantly pushing products in people's faces is going to feel like pressure—and in the end, it will only result in you driving people away.

If you want to have more success with your direct sales business, you need to focus on creating connections and relationships with people. Remember: it is called *network* marketing, meaning that you need to *network* to market. Creating catalogues and sales images are the company's job. *Promoting* them is your job. You can do that by creating meaningful relationships with people in your network and letting them come to the idea of purchasing all on their own.

There are many ways that you can connect with your audience and build a network without coming across as spammy or annoying. They are also directly supportive of your business, meaning that doing it this way is completely worth your while. These work both online and offline.

Online, you want to show off your lifestyle. Do not just show off your lifestyle in relation to the products and services that you are offering, but show it off in general. The key, however, is to stay focused on sharing the parts of your lifestyle that are still relevant and relatable to the ones in your ideal audience. This will ensure that they are paying attention and enjoying your content. Then, those few times that you do actually post with your products and invite people to learn more about them, you are going to be seen by your audience. You will also be more well-received because you have been spending time getting to know them and building a connection with them through previous posts, so they will feel more curious about this one. Experts say that online you want 80% of your posts creating relationships with your audience and only about 20% offering sales or inviting people to learn more about your business. Keeping this ratio in your online strategy will ensure that you are staying focused on networking more so than selling.

Offline, go about life as normal. Your focus should primarily be on connecting with more people and building relationships with them. If you can encourage people to follow you on social media or connect with you somewhere online, then what ends up happening is that they build chemistry with you before learning about what you do. Then, because they like you and they already know that you do not fit the identity of a pushy salesperson, they are more likely to pay attention and grow interested when they learn about your business.

If during the conversation you have the opportunity to talk about what you do for work or you can somehow bring your products into the conversation, make sure you do so in a way that proves that there's no pressure involved. In other words, let them ask the questions. If they ask what you do for work, simply respond with the name of your company, and let them know that you are an independent distributor for them. Do not go into a long sales pitch immediately after being asked. Instead, end with that bit of information, and let them ask you if they are interested in learning more.

Chapter 6: Presenting Your Opportunity to Prospects

Knowing how to properly present your opportunity to prospects is essential. The techniques I am going to show you in this chapter are going to support you in presenting products or services to prospective clients or presenting your business opportunity to prospective recruits. Both of these will follow the same general guidelines, so simply adjust your choice of words to accommodate for the presentation that you are making.

Invite Them to Approach You

Whenever someone shows interest in your business, always invite them to approach you. Online, this would include anyone who comments on your posts expressing interest. Offline, this would include anyone who expresses interest through a conversation that the two of you share together. After the initial interest has been expressed, always invite that person to contact you in a more private forum. Online, this could be moving the conversation to a private message. Offline, this could be calling you later or meeting for coffee for a more formal get together regarding the opportunity.

Inviting your prospect to approach you shows that you are not pushy and that the next move is in their hands. This allows them to feel in control and trust that you are not going to start spamming them with your offers and trying to push your product down their throat.

When you do invite them to approach you, particularly if the invite was made in person, always give them an idea of when you are generally available. This will not only give them the opportunity to contact you on their own terms but will also get an idea of when they could contact you in their mind. Then, they are already thinking about when to call you, so they are more likely to do so. This is a great way to invite a person to more conversation in a way that is not too passive but not too pressured, either.

Let Them Ask the Questions

During the conversation that you share with your prospect, let them ask the questions. You do not want your prospect to feel like you are interrogating them, so only ask questions if they are to support you in better answering your prospect's questions. For example, if they ask which product or service would be best for them, spend some time asking questions to learn more about what their needs are. Then, give them the solution.

If the conversation starts and continues with you asking all the questions, your prospect is going to start feeling overwhelmed. They do not want to be pitched on the idea; they want to explore it. Being pitched feels uncomfortable and carries too much pressure behind it. However, if you leave them open to explore the opportunity, and if you simply give answers as they ask or make yourself available to help them through their exploration, they feel in control. This helps them feel more comfortable and as though they are being respected by you during the process. As a result, they will remain interested and open to learning more about what you have to offer.

Lead The Conversation without Pressure

Although you want to let your prospect ask all of the questions, you still want to lead the conversation. After all, you are the expert. Gently guiding them toward the answers they need to purchase or join you is the best way to guide the conversation but without making it feel overwhelming. You can do this by offering answers that directly answer their question but begin guiding them to new thoughts that work toward the finalizing of the sale or recruitment.

For example, say your customer asks: "How do I know which financial solution is best for me?" You could answer, "Well, that really depends on what your needs are! Can you give me more information on what you feel you need most from your finances?" Then, when they give you their answer, you may begin telling them about how they can have those needs met by your solutions.

Guiding someone toward the solution rather than pushing them toward it will support you in closing more deals. This is because you are attracting them to the solution, making it seem more interesting and fulfilling to them. Furthermore, this form of guidance gives you plenty of opportunities to learn more about what their needs are and what solutions they would actually benefit from. Finding people the right solution is just as important as closing the opportunity, as this will ensure that they are satisfied with their choice after the deal is closed. That way, they are more likely to feel positive about it, and they will come back for more as a result.

Subtly Create a Sense of Urgency

When it comes to marketing you, always want to create a sense of urgency that encourages people to make a decision sooner rather than later. This is how you ensure that people continue thinking about you and that they do not simply forget because the offer was too passive or "it will be available later when I'm more ready."

Creating a subtle sense of urgency is how you can show people that there is urgency there but without creating pressure on them. For example, "Our September incentive ends in three days, so make sure you choose quickly!" is too much pressure. This is going to result in people feeling overwhelmed and likely looking for reasons to back out or purposefully wait longer just so that they can get away from the feeling of being pressured. Instead, say something like, "We still have three days left before this great incentive ends, so why don't you take a couple of days to think it over? Do you mind if I message you back in a day or two to see if you have any more questions I can answer for you?" This sentence proves the urgency of the offer in a way that lacks pressure and includes a request to follow up with your prospect. This means that they will spend more time thinking about it, will feel as though they are in control, and will look forward to hearing back from you so that you can help them make their decision.

Have a Resource Available for Them to Read Over

One great way to really help encourage prospects to purchase or join you is to have something for them to look at while they are thinking things through. A small handout, a write-up, a video, or any other form of resource that they can read over to learn more while they think things through is great. This resource should answer any basic questions they may have and give them the rundown on why the opportunity is one worth going for.

Giving people a resource is not only a great way to help them think things through, but it is also a wonderful no-pressure way to get information into their hands. This means that rather than going away and simply being left to their own thinking devices or having to look for other resources (and potentially find someone with more who communicates better with them,) they can look at yours. This keeps them operating as your prospect and interested in learning more from you and coming back to do business through you. As a result, you and your opportunity both stay fresh in their mind, making it more likely for them to choose in favor of closing the deal.

Always Request to Follow Up

Every single time you have a conversation with a prospect, always ask if you can follow up with them in a couple of days. This ensures that they are open to further communication and puts the power of the follow up in your hands. If you leave it in your prospects hands, they can easily forget, and then you lose a prospect. If you follow up too soon after not having set a clear expectation on if and when you would do so, then this follow-up can seem spammy. Instead, setting the expectations and taking the responsibility for the follow-up ensures that you are the one who will reach out. Through this, your prospect knows exactly when they can expect one, or they can adjust the date of when the follow-up would be accordingly.

When you take the responsibility for the follow-up, make sure that you always do just that. Never present your opportunity to a prospect and set the intention of a follow-up and then forget to do so. This can cost you a prospect and result in you not successfully closing the deal. Write the person's name down in your calendar on the date that the follow-up needs to happen, and make sure that you show up. This will ensure that you are readily available to continue presenting any information that they need to support them in making their decision.

Chapter 7: Converting Prospects into Distributors or Customers

After you have gotten to the point in the conversation where you are ready to start making your actual sales pitch, it is important that you do so in the right way. You do not want to spend plenty of time working toward creating a strong reputation with someone and building rapport only to blow it during the conversion.

There are various things that you need to take into consideration when it comes to converting prospects into distributors or customers. In this chapter, I am going to show you how to make the pitch itself and how to make sure that you are pitching the right thing that will adequately serve that person's needs. That way, you can make the conversion and do so with a solution that actually fulfills that prospect's needs, ensuring that they are satisfied and eager to continue on with the chosen solution and beyond.

Spend Time Getting to Know Your Pitch

It is always important that you have an idea of what you want to pitch to your prospect before you actually go into the conversation. If you are about to go into a follow-up conversation, spend the time between the initial point of contact and the follow-up curating a pitch specifically for that person. For the times where you need to pitch on the spot without a follow-up, have some form of pitch already practiced so that you know how to talk to the prospect without stumbling.

Spending time developing your pitch and getting to know it really well will ensure that when the time comes to actually make the pitch, you're ready. The worst thing you can do is go into a pitch unprepared and fumble over your words, apply too much or too little pressure, or leave information out because you were ill-prepared. Practicing in advance or at least making a mental note of what points you want to cover will ensure that you know exactly what you want to say and that you are ready to say it.

Early on, no matter how much you practice your pitch, it may still feel awkward. Furthermore, practicing a pitch without any experience as to what types of questions or statements people might have can be a challenge. As a result, some of your earliest pitches may not be your best work. Still, use this as an opportunity to get to know the pitch and to look for opportunities to make your pitch more effectively in the future. Make a note of what questions people typically have, what objections you are running into the most, and any other considerations that you feel you need to note in order to make your pitch effectively. Then, in the future, adjust your pitches to accommodate for these unique changes.

The more you practice, the easier it will be for you to curate pitches on the spot. This will come as a result of having a stronger idea of what the answers are to people's questions, feeling more confident in yourself, and having more practice in learning how to overcome common objections. As you grow more practiced, your pitches will become more candid and effective, which means you will begin getting greater results.

Even though you already know that your earliest pitches may not be your best ones, it is imperative that you prepare and practice. You have to start somewhere, and there is only one way that you can get better at something. Be prepared to pitch, and be prepared to do so often. This is an essential part of growth, so using this tool and leveraging it effectively will ensure that you achieve great results.

Initiate the Conversation with a Question

You never want to jump straight into the pitch when you are selling something to someone. This comes across as pushy and tacky. It also shows that you are not considerate about the other person's concerns. This can leave a bad impression on people, resulting in a quick and immediate "no" and a damaged reputation.

Instead, start the conversation with a question. If you are following up with someone who you have already chatted with and who has already been considering the opportunity, open with something like "Hey (name)! I'm just following up from the other day. Have you had a chance to think about (opportunity) yet?" This is a simple conversation starter that gets the conversation immediately focused on what you are working toward without sounding pushy or inconsiderate.

If you haven't had a conversation yet with the person, and this is your first one, you want to start the conversation with a question that gets the person thinking and talking about your opportunity. Something like "Hey (name)! I see that you are interested in (opportunity), and I just wanted to reach out and see if there were any questions you might have about it?" This is a simple and open question that invites the person to ask about anything they may be curious about. As a result, the conversation gets started, and the ball gets rolling so that you can eventually move into your pitch.

Answer Any Questions Your Prospect Might Have

Before you *ever* make a pitch to *anyone*, make sure you have the information that you need to do so. If you are not considerate about your prospect, you are not going to convert them into a distributor or customer. It simply won't happen. People like to do business with people who are considerate and compassionate, not people who are pushy and who seem like they are just trying to close a deal.

Instead of prematurely making your pitch, take some time, and get to know the person and their needs. Pay attention to what matters to them, what they are looking for, and what can really support them in making a decision. Ask them if they have any questions, and make it clear that they are always welcome to come to you if they need support or are looking for more answers. Serving your prospects instead of selling to your prospects will ensure that they feel accommodated for and considered. As a result, they will realize that you are compassionate and genuinely interested in creating great results for them using your opportunity.

Only once you know that you already have all of the information and that they have asked all of their outstanding questions should you then move into a pitch. However, you do not want to accidentally draw the question period out too long before you move into the pitch. Doing that could result in them losing interest and not paying attention, or talking themselves out of it altogether.

The best way to tell that someone is ready to be pitched to is by the amount of interest they have in your opportunity and the initiative that they are showing. If they are asking you more about the products and are showing interest in hearing about the opportunity, then you can begin pitching. Alternatively, if they begin answering questions with similar answers or by tying them back into other answers (i.e. saying things like, "as I said before..."), then you know that you want to move toward the pitch so that you don't bore them or make them feel like you are not listening.

Even after you are confident that your prospect has asked all of their questions, always make it clear that they can come to you at any time if they have more concerns. This includes during the process, afterward, or at any time in the future. Letting them know that you are always available to support them helps them feel confident that if they have anything else that they desire to ask, you will be there to support them in finding the answers they need. This shows that you are service-based and focused on giving them the best experience possible, making your prospect feel supported and cared for and more likely to want to do business with you again.

Make Your Pitch

Once everything else has been done, you are ready to make your pitch. Here is where you want to begin using what you had already practiced. That way, you make sure that you have included all of the information required to support your prospect in making their official decision.

When you open the pitch, always make it clear that you have been listening to their needs and that you feel you have a great opportunity or offer that is going to fulfill what they are looking for. Then, let them know what the opportunity is and why you think it would fit their needs. End your pitch with a question that invites them to engage back with you so that the pitch does not sound like the end of a conversation.

It is important that you do not make your pitch too long or drawn out. Using what is called an "elevator" pitch is a great way to begin pitching your opportunity to people because it supports you in giving just enough information and then only giving more when your prospect shows interest in knowing more. These pitches generally start with one to two lines about the opportunity, followed by a question. Then, if they ask for more information, you can add in more and let them know further details about the opportunity.

Below is a great example of how you can make a pitch to recruit someone using the elevator pitch style.

You: "You mentioned that you are looking for a way to earn extra income so that you can cover your bills easier, and I know that you are passionate about health. The company I am with offers incredible health products that can support people in achieving their wellness goals and feeling more empowered about their health. I really think this would tie in great with your needs and passions! Does this opportunity interest you?"

Prospect: "Yes, that does sound like a great idea!"

You: "Great! The company is seriously incredible; I know you will love it! Right now, we have an exclusive offer to join the company for just $99! With that, you get all of the marketing materials you need to get started, plus some great products for you to share with your market. I also have a great online community where I offer training and support to distributors with goals just like yours! Would you like me to send you the sign-up link and help you get started?"

Prospect: "Yes please!"

As you can see, formatting the pitch in this way supports the person in getting information but without feeling overloaded. If you were to go too far into detail with information by sending every single detail over right away, you might overwhelm your prospect and leave them not wanting to answer you. Instead, giving only the information that is relevant to the point of the conversation that you are at can support you in making the pitch in a way that keeps your prospect engaged and interested. Then, they can make the decision, and you can offer to help walk them through the process if they choose to join you!

The same general concept goes to selling products. While you will not be making the pitch based on the business opportunity, you will be making it based on the product or service that your prospect is interested in. Presenting the information in the same way but based on your product or service offer will ensure that your prospect has the information that they need to make their decision and that you can close the deal.

Chapter 8: Creating A Strong Follow-Up System

Following up with people is an essential way of making sure that every single lead you generate is tapped. If you spend all of your time marketing and generating new leads, and then you do not take the time to actually follow up with those leads, you are wasting your time. Many potential customers or distributors can slip through your fingers and find their way to another distributor if you are not paying attention and making use of a strong follow-up system.

Creating a follow-up system does not have to be challenging or overdone. Instead, a simple follow-up system can be created that makes it easy to follow and effective. In fact, when it comes to a follow-up system, the easier it is, the more effective it becomes. I am going to show you how you can take advantage of both automatic and manual follow-up systems to ensure that you successfully follow up with every single lead that you generate. Making use of both of these styles will ensure that no one slips through the cracks and that you are regularly nurturing your leads so that your network continues to grow and convert.

When to Use Automated Follow-ups

Automated follow-ups are a great way to follow up with people who enjoy following your online presence and who opt in to staying up to date. The most common way to do automated follow-ups is through using an e-mail list.

Your automated follow-up system is going to come into use anytime someone lands on your website or is directed to sign up to your newsletter by you in the online space. For example, if you have a blog, you can capture emails on it through a pop-up that encourages people to sign up for your email newsletter. Alternatively, if you are on Facebook, you might consider leaving a link where people can sign up to stay up to date and receive great information regarding your industry and the products or services that you offer. Some companies have newsletters that have already been designed for you and that are sent out by your company from anyone who signs up on your consultant website. These can be great, as they capture emails and put them directly into a list and cover the marketing part for you so that you don't have to. However, they are created by the company themselves, so they will lack your personal branding and tone of voice.

Using email lists is a great way to allow people to choose to be followed up with and to continue receiving follow-ups to their inbox every time a new newsletter goes out. These types of prospects are willingly choosing to be followed up with and are opting to see the new newsletter each time it comes out. As a result, they are considered to be warm leads because they are showing so much interest in your opportunity.

When to Use Manual Follow-ups

Manual follow-ups are the best way to follow up on a more personal level. This is how you can follow up with someone whom you have already chatted with about your opportunity and who wants to know more about what you have to offer. You can follow up with people manually any time you have had a personal conversation with them.

Using manual follow-ups is more intimate and focused specifically on the person that you are following up with. Through this type of follow-up, you have the unique opportunity to answer questions and make yourself personally available to your prospect so that you can support them in making their decision. Manual follow-ups are a great way to generate hot leads because these are people who are asking you to update them. As a result, they are more likely to purchase from you. Furthermore, you can curate your information and pitch just for them, making it more effective for that person specifically. When you have the opportunity to do so, always use manual follow up with individual people. That way, you have more control over the situation, and you can close the deal with greater ease.

How to Create an Automated Follow-up System

Setting up an automated follow-up system requires three aspects: a lead-generator, a place where you capture emails, and a platform from which you send your emails. With these three components in place, you have everything you need to encourage people to opt-in and to receive your newsletters through their emails.

Lead-generators or opt-in incentives are something that people offer as a way to encourage them to sign up for their email list. If you choose to make a lead-generator, which you absolutely should, you want to make something that is going to be relevant to your audience. A short e-book, a workbook, a checklist, an exclusive training video, or any other form of inexpensive but valuable freebie that you can offer is a great way to give people an incentive to join your mailer list.

Once they have joined, the person should then receive the item directly to their inbox, or they should land on the page where the freebie is offered. Most web hosting companies like WordPress or Squarespace, as well email newsletter platforms like MailChimp or ConvertKit, will give you all of the tools that you need to ensure that your new subscriber receives their promised gift. They should also be able to walk you through the process of creating your opt-in page or pop up so that people have a spot where they can opt-in for your freebie and receive your newsletter.

Lastly, all you need to do is create great email newsletters and send them out on a regular basis! For automated newsletters, ideally, you want to be sending a new email once per week. This way, you can update your subscribers on weekly deals, give them great new tips or advice that is specific to your niche, and invite them to message you back. When you email your subscribers once per week, you ensure that you are not overwhelming them so that they unsubscribe and you also ensure that you are emailing them enough that they actually remember who you are and what offer you have for them.

How to Create a Manual Follow-up System

Manual follow-up systems are extremely simple. Essentially, you want to get the person's best method of contact and write it down. Then, make sure you write down their name, too. You can also include a note on how to pronounce it if it is a particularly challenging name so that you do not accidentally mispronounce it during your follow-up. Then, you need to note in your calendar what date you need to update them on.

It is also a good idea to write down some notes regarding what it is that you are following up on and what their particular needs or concerns are. This ensures that you do not forget about what they have already told you and that you are readily prepared to go into the follow-up conversation. This also proves that they matter enough to you, that you took the time to remember their needs and to pay attention to what they have told you.

Since manual follow up is quite straightforward, there really is nothing special that you need to know other than to write down their information and then get in touch with them when you have promised to. This is definitely the simplest form of follow-up, though it can be time-consuming if you have many people to update.

Make sure that, if for some reason, you cannot follow up on the date that you agreed you would, at least make contact with that person. Do not simply leave them waiting. If you can, give them a quick call or message, and ask how they have been doing and if they've had a chance to think things over. If they respond that they have, rather than going into the pitch or using this particular follow-up to move into the offer, use it to book your next follow-up. That way, your prospect knows that you have not forgotten about them and can look forward to connecting with you again. Leaving a prospect without answers and not connecting with them when you said you would leave a bad impression about how you do business. It can also result in them not wanting to do business with you for fear of being abandoned or not having access to the support that they need.

Knowing When to Stop Following Up

Sometimes, you might find yourself following up with someone who seems to be going nowhere. They may have initially been a prospect—but after a few attempted follow-ups, the conversation seems to go nowhere, or they are showing a lack of interest in what you are offering. If this happens, it is important that you know when to stop following up with them. Generally, after three follow-ups that do not advance to anything more than disinterested conversation or with a conversation that feels like you have to put too much work into to get any answers from the other person, you can stop.

Following up with someone who is disinterested too many times can result in them growing annoyed with you and unfollowing or unfriending you. Furthermore, it is a waste of your time, as it will not result in anything positive. Even if you do eventually get them to make up their mind and purchase from you or join you, the amount of work that you are going to have to put into keeping them is going to be too much. Plus, if they join you, they will be unlikely to do anything with their opportunity because they simply are not motivated enough. Instead of wasting your time following up with people who are not interested, move on to people who genuinely are.

Chapter 9: Building an Effective Downline

Since a large part of your income in MLM is based on your downline and their performance, knowing how to build an effective downline is important. You need to make sure that you are finding the right prospects who are actually going to take advantage of the business opportunity and turn it into something successful for themselves and for you.

In this chapter, I am going to show you how to qualify prospects to discover who is going to be a strong downline support and who is going to stay most dedicated to their goals. Finding downlines who are qualified in this way will ensure that you are finding people who are committed to success. As a result, your whole team will grow more powerful.

Finding Prospects for Your Downline

Part of building your downline is knowing where to find prospects. Prospects can come from all over the place, though the most common place to find prospects is on social media. Through your engagement and attraction marketing efforts, people are naturally going to start looking toward you to learn more about the opportunity that you have to offer them. The more you share about yourself and how your company is changing your life, the more your prospects are going to start showing up and seeking information from you about joining your company.

The best way to continue searching for prospects is to continue posting and to engage with every single person who interacts with your posts. If you have people who tend to engage a great deal or who show interest, do the same and begin engaging more on their posts, too. This helps you develop a relationship with that person, which is going to help set the tone for you to attract them to your business even more.

When people start noticing how much your business is changing your life and how much fun you are having, they are going to start asking you questions about the opportunity. Then, all you have to do is have your initial and follow-up conversation, and then give them your pitch to get them on board. This is quite simple. In fact, it is the easiest way to get new prospects joining your company.

People who approach you and who put this level of initiative into joining your company are the ones who are most likely to be self-starters. This proves that they are going to be willing to do what it takes to generate success and achieve their goals in the MLM industry. As a result, they are more likely to remain active consultants who will help your own position within the company grow as they continue to grow as well.

Another way that you can meet prospects is through gaining referrals. If you have clients whom you love and who have been purchasing from you for a while, ask them if they are willing to refer their friends to you that might be interested in what you are doing. If they have any friends who show interest in your industry or in making extra money, then, they can refer them to you, and you can show them the opportunity.

Prospects can show up virtually anywhere, too. You never know when you are going to have a conversation with a person who is going to be interested in doing something like you are doing. Always keep your eyes open for an opportunity to let someone know that you have an offer they might be interested in. Then, give them the information that they need to contact you, and invite them to do just that. Remember: you do not want to be pushy, but you always want to make sure that you are putting the offer out there.

Engaging with Your Prospective Downline

Once you have met someone who might be interested in becoming a part of your team, it is a good idea that you begin engaging with your prospect. This is a great way to begin getting to know who they are, so as to get an idea of what their interests and goals are, and to discover if they would actually be a good fit to your company. You can also use this time to let them know more, too, to see if they feel interested as well.

As you engage with your prospective downline, make sure that you are taking the time to sell them on the idea. You do not want to approach the subject too passively, or this can result in them thinking that the idea is not worth their time or excitement. Instead, share some success stories with them, and let them know how much there is to be excited about. This is a great way to show them that there is plenty to look forward to within the business should they choose to join.

You can also focus on sharing how helpful your team is and how easy it is to succeed when you have so many people working together to help you. This is something that many people look forward to with MLM businesses. Oftentimes, people joining MLM companies have never run their own business before. As a result, the idea of having to do everything on their own may seem intimidating or scary. Letting them know that there is a strong system of support awaiting them is a great way to prove that they will not have to do everything on their own. Focus on emphasizing how close your team is and how much they truly do help each other work toward succeeding in achieving their own goals.

Make sure that as you are sharing this conversation with your prospect that you allow the conversation to follow a natural path. You do not want it to seem like the only thing you can talk about is the opportunity. Let them know that you are a real human and that you have other interests, too. If they steer the conversation toward something like hobbies or family, for example, do not be afraid to follow the conversation down that route. Then, after a few sentences back and forth on that subject, find a way to tie it back into the opportunity. For example, you could bring it back to the topic of your business by mentioning how you being with this company has impacted your family.

It is important that you spend just as much time building a relationship with prospects as you do selling them on the opportunity. If they are joining you, chances are one of the biggest reasons is because they want to be able to earn more money and have access to the support that comes with being with an MLM company. Prove that there is plenty of support, personal connection, and training involved by being willing to show them that right from the very start.

One thing people tend to do wrong is starting relationships out on the wrong foot. Your first impression truly does matter. You want to develop a reputation of being someone who cares and who puts people first, rather than someone who is simply trying to recruit as many people as possible. When people realize how compassionate you are and how much you care about the work you do, they will be far more likely to join you.

Qualifying Your Downline to Find the Best Team Members

While you probably won't want to deny anyone who asks to join your team, it is a good idea that you take the time to qualify the prospects that you want to pursue your team. Qualifying your prospects is the best way to make sure that you are building your team up with inspiring, empowering, and motivated people who are going to do their best to generate success with their business. It also ensures that you do not waste your time trying to recruit people who are not going to do anything with the opportunity anyway, as they do not end up earning your team any growth or income in the end.

Qualifying people requires you to look for four main characteristics in each person that you are pursuing to join your team: drive, goals, a positive personality, and the ability to connect with other people. When a person has these four characteristics then you can guarantee that they already have a great deal of what it takes to succeed. With the right training and support, these are the types of prospects who go on to become team leaders that rapidly climb the ranks and generate success for themselves.

These are the people that are going to take what you give them and run with it, so they are the ones that you want to be investing your time into. Not only are you going to have the blessing of watching your own business grow, then, but you will also get to watch someone else's. When you are operating a company that relies so much on having a team, such as with an MLM company, seeing your entire team succeed is exciting and inspiring. This will motivate you to do better, and it will motivate them to do better as well. As a result, you all get to win because each of you is taking the time required to invest in yourselves and your businesses.

Chapter 10: Leading Your Team Members Effectively

Knowing how to lead your downline is an important process of building your business. Having a strong team is a part of what makes working with an MLM company so attractive. People love having that support and community and knowing that they can rely on others who are working towards similar goals as they are. Having people that they can relate to and develop connections within this way inspires them to continue working and to stay motivated in achieving their goals.

If you want to generate the type of team that stays focused on success and that continues moving forward, you need to set the tone and be the person that guides the team in this direction. You can do this by developing a service-based leadership that is going to allow you to show up and is there to support your team. This will also help your team grow into the team culture that you are developing through your leadership, ensuring that everyone contributes to the supportive, compassionate, and motivating environment that you are building for them.

The Importance of Service-Based Leadership

Service-based leadership is one that is designed to stay focused on how you can help your team do better. Rather than simply leading in the way that you believe leadership is needed, you lead in a manner that your team needs you to lead. Being a service-based leader means that you need to stay receptive to your team's feedback so that you can continue leading in a way that serves them.

When you lead in a service-based leadership style, only three things remain consistent: support, communication, and adaptation. Your primary focus should always revolve around supporting your team to do better so that they can build their businesses and continue to achieve success. This helps them stay motivated and committed, keeping them working at their businesses for a long time to come. You can maintain this level of support by communicating frequently. When you communicate often, you can listen to their needs and make yourself available as needed. Lastly, you need to know how to adapt. The needs of your team will change from time to time, and you need to know how to adapt your leadership style and approach to ensure that you fulfill these needs as they change. As long as you continue working to support, communicate with, and adapt to your team's needs, you can guarantee that your downline is going to grow strong and unstoppable.

'Be A Leader, Not a Boss

When it comes to leading a team it is essential that you learn to be a leader and not a boss. Remember: these individuals are all people who, like you, want to do their own thing. They value their freedom, the feeling of being in control, and their right to do things their way. This is one of the big attractions of network marketing. That being said, do not be the person that tries to take that away by attempting to lead your team like you are their boss. You are not. You are their leader.

The best way you can lead people is to show them through your own actions and to coach them when it is needed. When you are a role model that they can look up to, your downline can easily look to you for support and inspiration. They will want to come to you for assistance because they will trust that they can get support from you when it is needed. Your downline will also know that when they seek you out, they are going to be shown how to do things, not told. This means that they are going to really get the opportunity to learn how to do their best so that they can achieve the same type of success that you are aiming for. Remember: you are all here to be your own bosses. Lead your team so that they know how to be the best boss to themselves that they can be.

Learn How to Manage Your Time

As your team continues to grow, the demands on your time will continue to grow as well. Learning how to effectively manage your time from the start is a powerful way to make sure that you are never wasting time, losing time, or running out of time. Every single conversation you have with a member of your team should be productive and focused. Stay clear on what the point of the conversation is, and stay on topic. The more focused you are, the easier it is to reach your goal and move on to your next order of business.

This also goes for when you are doing training calls, orientations, and other similar events. If you are in any forum where you are talking to a large number of people all at once, make sure that you stay on topic and that you are clearly focused on your results. Getting off topic or taking too long to communicate the point to your audience will bore them and result in them not listening to you. If they stop listening, you're not leading effectively. Be the type of leader who gets to the point, not the one who loses everyone's interest and fails to lead.

Stay Consistent in Your Leadership

As you develop your leadership style, make sure that you stay consistent. Your team will not appreciate having you being unreliable and inconsistent when they are trying to look up to you for support and motivation. Be consistent in the tasks you do as a leader, in the training you offer, and in the way that you motivate and inspire people. Show up every single day, and give the same level of commitment (or more) every single day. This shows people that you are dedicated and motivated and that they can rely on you.

You also want to make sure that you are training your downline on the importance of consistency. Teach them how to take baby steps towards generating success rather than pushing them to try and sprint to the finish line. Running a business requires time and patience, so demonstrating this and teaching it to your downline is important. If you want, you can create a resource that outlines the baby steps they need to be taking to succeed and offer it to each person in your downline. Then, they each have access to what they need so that they know what step to take next and where to go in each moment.

Keep The Lines of Communication Open

Nothing is more challenging than trying to work with a leader who is unapproachable or does not communicate with their team. When you are leading your team, make sure that you keep your lines of communication open. This allows your team to know that there is support available to them whenever they need it.

As your downline grows, you might find that making yourself available around the clock is virtually impossible. Trying to get back to that many people or trying to stay up to date with everyone can be a challenge. Still, communication is important. In this situation, there are a few things that you can do to maintain your open communication but without taking away from your own time or overwhelming your schedule too much. The first one is to have set days or hours that you are available to share with your downline. This is when they can contact you or expect a response from you if they have contacted you. That way, everyone knows when you are available and does not grow frustrated or annoyed if you do not message them outside of those times.

Another thing that you can do if your team is growing particularly large is to have a set day or days each week that you will go live on your team's Facebook group and invite your downline to join you. Then, they can ask questions, and you can update them on anything that is going on in the business through that video. This is a great way to show your team your face and let them know that a real person is leading their team. It builds relationships between you and your team members and keeps the communication open.

Lastly, if your team is too big for you to lead alone, you might consider picking a couple of other leaders on your team to help you lead the team. Picking people who know the company well, who have shown the initiative, and who are leading their own downlines is a great way to make sure that you have enough people available to help anyone who may have questions. Make sure that your entire team knows who is being added to the leadership and that there is a document or note available somewhere that lets them know how they can contact leaders and if any of the leaders have a set time when they are able to be contacted. This way, everyone knows who to go to and when.

Encourage Your Downline to Leverage Their Strengths

When it comes to leading people, it is essential that you teach people how to recognize their strengths and leverage them for their businesses. Inspiring people to see how great they are and how successful they are with certain activities is an incredible way to motivate people and keep them moving forward.

In addition to having people come to know their own strengths, take the time to recognize their strengths, too. Watch your downline in action, and do not be afraid to celebrate them for their achievements. Write posts in your team group about how awesome they are, highlighting their achievements, or celebrating them for doing a job well done. There isn't a need to be any special occasion for celebrating people. Simply celebrating people just because is a great way to keep the team's morale up and positivity pumping so that everyone stays motivated to do their best.

As people grow to know and leverage their strengths, they will also come to understand what their weaknesses are. Then, if need be, you can coach them on how to overcome these weaknesses so that they can continue to develop a strong business. If you notice that many people share a similar weakness, you might consider doing specific training on how they can overcome these weaknesses so that they can experience greater success.

Train, Inspire, and Motivate

As a leader, the best things that you can offer to your downline is training, inspiration, and motivation. Make sure that these three things are included in how you lead your team. Focus on leading them with the intention of showing them how they can do their best, inspiring them to feel confident in their ability to do their best, and motivating them to put the effort into proving to themselves that they can make it happen.

A great way to keep these three components active in your team is to include them in your specific leadership schedule. In other words, every week or month have some form of training in the group where you or another leader will come on and train the rest of the group on how to do something. This does not necessarily have to be someone who is leading your team, either. Inviting any team member who has something to teach or even inviting guest speakers to chat with your team is a great way to begin building up your team and teaching them how to do their best. Make sure that these trainings always include motivation and inspiration, too, to encourage your team to keep moving forward.

Chapter 11: Handling Rejection like a Pro

Rejection is an inevitable part of a business. At the end of the day, no matter how awesome your offer is or how much you think it would work for someone else, some people just won't be interested. When you experience rejection in your business, it is essential that you handle it properly. Handled properly, rejection is not necessarily the means to an end. Instead, it may be an opportunity to prove that you have integrity and that you can respect others. As a result, the person who have rejected you may just become the same person who refers your next best prospect to you.

Detach from the Outcome Before You Even Start

If you go into every single prospect or presentation with an attachment to how you think it is going to turn out, then chances are you are going to feel a lot more hurt when things don't work out. Instead of setting yourself up to feel bad every time something doesn't work out, set yourself up to succeed. Detach from the outcome, and let things flow naturally.

Detaching from the outcome ensures that you are not so fixated on your desired results, that you end up too narrow sighted to see other opportunities that may arise, too. When you go into anything with an attachment toward how you want it to end, you can pretty much guarantee that you are going to experience being let down in one way or another. You will either feel disappointed in the rejection itself or not realize that many opportunities came of it, or you will be so fixed on having your outcome, that you may not realize that an even better one presented itself. As a result, you can miss out on many opportunities that actually could pan out because you are too busy worrying about what hadn't.

When you go into anything, rather than having an attachment to the outcome, set a goal. When you do, set the goal loosely. Set an intention that you are going to get the best results possible and that these results are, in one way or another, going to support your business growing to be bigger than it already is. This ensures that you head into every single opportunity with a clear mind and a focus on having the best possible outcome, rather than a specific one.

Consider Asking Why They Rejected Your Offer

Whenever someone rejects your offer or opportunity, never be afraid to ask why. Asking for the reason is a great way to discover if there was anything that you could have done differently or anything that you should have paid attention to beforehand. Feedback is always a great way to discover where you can do better, how you can grow, and how you can emphasize your success.

When you do ask for someone to let you know why they have rejected your offer, make sure that you go into it ready to receive feedback. You might end up learning that something you did was the very reason why they said no in the end. This can feel painful because you never want to think that you made a mistake that cost you a prospect. However, realize that in taking the time to listen to this feedback, you can learn how to approach your sales more effectively so that you will have an easier time recruiting new prospects in the future.

Sometimes, people may not want to offer you feedback, or the feedback that they offer you might be unproductive or even unkind. In these situations, do not press for more information or get into an argument with the other person. Instead, end the conversation, and release what they have said. This will allow you to let go of the situation and move on so that you can continue growing your business. If what a person says results in you feeling unmotivated or discouraged, take this time to practice your mindset skills so that you can give yourself a pep talk and move on.

Refrain from Investing Your Emotions into It

When it comes to business, people rarely make decisions based on their emotions. Instead, they make them based off of ration, reason, and logic. Make sure that you do not come into decisions very emotionally invested. Doing so can result in you feeling personally invested in the outcome and emotionally involved to the point that it feels like a personal attack on you when people reject you. As a consequence, you may find yourself feeling very emotional after any rejection.

While you do not want to run your business with a lack of passion, you also want to refrain from becoming so emotionally invested, that it is a challenge for you to remain level-headed and focused when challenges come up. Instead, be invested enough that you can show off your passion but be detached enough that your emotions do not feel personally attacked anytime someone rejects you.

In addition, you also want to refrain from bringing your emotions into any business dealing to avoid having any emotional outbursts. If you are particularly emotionally invested in an outcome, handling rejection can be much harder. People who do not check their emotions properly can end up having an argument or another unprofessional outburst with someone, which can result in you not only losing the prospect but also losing your reputation. If you handle rejection in this way, people are going to think that you are unprofessional and not a good person to do business with. Instead of looking for your support, they will be afraid that you will have the same response toward them.

Do Not Look at Rejection as a Means to an End

Rejection is not always the means to an end. In fact, in most cases, rejection can be seen as a positive thing. When someone rejects you and then the two of you never share an interaction again, in many cases, you have been given a blessing. Someone who wants to reject you but chooses to join you because they are afraid of saying no can end up being a waste of time in the end. This has nothing to do with the person or their character but rather the fact that they are not the type of prospect that's going to help generate more success within your business.

Another thing to realize is that when you get rejected, this does not mean that the person does not think your product has value or is interesting. Instead, it simply means that they are not interested themselves. Perhaps it does not fit in with their lifestyle or budget, so they decide that they are not interested. However, if you respect them and you treat that person with dignity and kindness, you can feel confident that if they do meet someone who would be interested, they might just refer them your way. That's right—the very people who reject you might be the same ones to refer some of the best clients your way. Always look on the bright side!

Handle Rejection with Poise, Grace, and Integrity

When it comes to handling rejection, always make sure that you do so with poise and grace. Consider what your reputation is and act accordingly. Use manners, show respect, and maintain your integrity during the entire conversation. Never behave in a way that makes the person question whether or not they were right to have even contacted you or given you the time to pitch in the first place. If you do, you will leave a bad impression over who you are.

They say that when it comes to business, people show their true colors when they are rejected or when they face hard times. Knowing how to handle your rejections with poise, grace, and integrity will ensure that you show people that you can handle these moments with dignity. As a result, they will have greater respect for you. This means that even though you lose a prospect, you do not lose your reputation, too.

Make Sure You Respect Yourself

In any instance of rejection, always take the time to respect yourself. If you are disrespected during the process of being rejected, or if anyone tries to treat you poorly during the process, do not take it. You are not required to argue your worth to anyone. Instead, politely end the conversation and call it a day.

Unfortunately, sometimes in business, you are going to face people who have very little respect for other people. If you do not take the time to learn how to respect yourself and apply it, you might find yourself failing in your business based on the mean words of a bully. This is a tragic way to let your business fail. Do not let the harsh words of an unkind person bring you down, and do not stoop so low as to respond to them. You owe yourself the respect of refusing that kind of treatment and moving on from the conversation. Furthermore, you are your own boss, and you have every right to demand that you be treated with respect in every single conversation. If you are not, you do not have to engage in that conversation—period. This is true even for conversations with people who are paying you or bringing money into your business. It may be challenging, but do not be afraid to stand up for yourself. You deserve it.

Chapter 12: Why Some People Don't Make Money?

Chances are that you have heard of many stories where people join MLM companies, sell for a little while, exhaust their market quickly, and then quit. It is not uncommon to have these same people tell you about how it is basically impossible to make any money with an MLM business and that you are better off doing something else. The reality is that you actually can make a great deal of money with your business. However, there are some fatal mistakes that people make that result in them not making any money. As a result, these people never succeed.

The truth is there are many people who will never make it in an MLM company. This is because they do not have what it takes. They are not devoted enough and do not have the drive to continue trying, and they are unwilling to learn about how to turn this venture into a successful and profitable source of income. This does not mean that they are bad people—just that they are not cut out for making money in the MLM industry. Making money through MLM does require you to take the time to learn about what you are actually doing and commit to doing better all the time. If you do not invest that kind of time and commitment into your business, you can pretty much guarantee that you will fail.

I want to give you the main reasons why people do not make money in MLM companies and what you can do to make sure that you are not one of these people. This way, you can feel confident that you will not make the same mistakes that they did and that you will instead be able to succeed in your business and be one of the many millionaires produced by the MLM industry.

They Don't Have Enough Focus

It is not uncommon for people to join network marketing businesses and assume that they will be easy because it is all laid out in front of them. They want their friend or acquaintance make it look easy, and they assume that they simply need to buy the kit and make a few posts—and then sales will come rolling in. When things don't happen right away, they begin to lose focus, and they quit before they've even really had a chance to get things rolling.

When you start your network marketing business, it is essential that you commit to staying focused and working on your business every single day. If your consistency falters, and you stop showing up, you can pretty much guarantee that you are going to fail in your business.

They Never Learned How to Market Properly

Unfortunately, a lot of negative and ineffective marketing strategies are promoted in MLM companies. People who are not really clear on what effective marketing strategies are teach other people how to market in a way that is unproductive. As a result, many MLM distributors end up marketing in a way that is tacky, pushy, and ineffective. Because people typically only respond poorly to these tactics if they even bother to respond at all, it can result in the distributor quitting before they ever actually got anywhere with their business.

It is essential that you understand that you are working as a professional marketer when you become a distributor. This means that you need to read up on how to market effectively and discover what it actually takes to market. This way, you can attract clients to you rather than push them away by marketing in a way that makes them annoyed and uninterested.

They Didn't Position Themselves as a Leader

As a distributor that is selling a product or service, people want to know that you know what you are talking about. If a person who is selling does not sell with authority and confidence, people are going to start assuming that their products are probably not that great.

Alternatively, they may not feel confident enough in the distributor to purchase from them. Instead, they may prefer to go to a different one who is going to be more productive and helpful.

When you join an MLM company, make a clear and honest effort to know everything that you can about the business, the industry, and any trends that may be rising in it. Knowing everything you can ensures that you can market yourself as an expert, and people feel confident in coming to you and asking you any questions they might have.

They Didn't Target Their Niche Effectively

When people market but are not clear and specific in who they are marketing to, no one ends up listening. Marketing heavily relies on people relating to you and your message. However, when people are not specific in their message, they end up sharing things that are not really that relatable. People want to feel like they can personally relate on a deep level when they are reading things. This is how they stay interested. This is also how they know that the product or service is specifically meant for them.

When you are marketing to people, refrain from being too vague in your marketing. It can be tempting to try and market to an entire industry, but this is not effective. You will end up washing yourself out and not being recognized as someone who actually knows what they are doing. Instead, stay focused and market specifically. You will get way more engagement, and you will grow far faster.

They Tried to Make Things Too Complicated

People who are not really sure of what it takes to run a business have a tendency to overcomplicate things. One of the reasons that they join an MLM business is because everything is clearly set out for them, and it is easy for them to identify exactly what needs to be done. However, once they begin, they start trying to do things in a way that makes it far too complicated. As a result, they struggle to find new prospects and convert them because they are trying to do way more than they actually need to.

Instead of trying to overcomplicate things, focus on making things as simple as possible—the easier, the better. Avoid letting your boredom or impatience get the best of you, as this can quickly result in you trying to do more to fill the time. All that will end up happening is you fill your time with activities that kill your business. Don't do that.

They Got Impatient

MLM success stories are filled with people who got rich, but very few people actually take the time to realize what it took to get there or how long. As a result, people have this illusion that joining an MLM company means that they are going to get rich quick and that it will be easy. This is not the case. As with any other industry, building a strong MLM company requires you to take your time and be patient. The stronger of a foundation you build, the stronger of a company you are going to have. However, if you are not willing to put in that time, which most people aren't, it can result in quitting before you ever actually create any success.

Instead of getting into an MLM business assuming that you are going to be wildly successful and then growing impatient and quitting before you even get there, slow down. Be realistic about what you want and what it is going to take for you to get there. Find a way that you can keep yourself busy during those times when you feel bored or impatient, and stay focused on what the end result is going to be. This will keep you from quitting before you ever have the chance to become successful.

They Chose to Blame Others for Their Mistakes or Failures

When people get into an MLM company, and they do not start seeing the results they want within a specific period of time, it is not uncommon to see people starting to blame those around them—that, or they will begin to blame circumstances. It happens all the time: a person joins an MLM thinking it will be great and then proceeds to blame the economy, the industry, their team, or clients for not helping them become successful. So, thinking that they have done their best and that there was nothing else they could have possibly done, they quit and move on.

This is a huge mistake. First off, if you ever fail in any business, you have to be willing to shoulder the responsibility. In the end, it comes down to you not taking the time to learn what goes into making the business a success and then committing to the business until success happens for you. It has nothing to do with anything other than you. If you choose a company that's unable to help you generate success, that is because you haven't done your research. If prospects do not convert to clients, that is because you've never stopped to learn how to help them convert. If you have not generated the income you want, it is because you haven't done what you need to in order to generate that income.

This can sound harsh, but being willing to shoulder the responsibility is actually empowering. When you realize that the only person who is capable of helping you fail or succeed is you, then you realize that all of the power is in your hands. As a result, there is absolutely no reason why you cannot make your business work and generate the level of income that you desire.

They Never Actually Wanted to Succeed

Lastly, a big reason that people fail in their businesses is that they never actually wanted to succeed. This may sound crazy when you think about it, but truthfully, not everyone goes into their business with a strong desire to succeed. Some go in without any intention of doing anything with the opportunity. Some simply want the goodies that come in the kit or the potential for the opportunity to be there if they decide they want to. And some will go into it because they feel like they are being pressured. Not everyone joins an MLM company because they want to succeed or because they believe they can.

The only way to overcome this is to make sure that you go in with a strong intention and clear reason to your actions. If you go into your business and do not stay focused and dedicated to your commitment, then you may not have actually been that devoted to succeeding in the first place. The only way you can fix that is to look inside and figure out what have made you lose interest.

Conclusion

Congratulations on finishing *Insanely Effective Network and Multi-Level Marketing for Introverts on Social Media*!

The very fact that you have read the entire book proves that you are clearly dedicated to making your network marketing business a success. I hope that in reading this book, you felt that you were able to find all of the resources that you needed in order to truly generate the success that you desire.

Building a network marketing business and earning an income is a powerful way of taking your earnings into your own hands and living the kind of life that you want to live. When you do this, you give yourself an unlimited earning potential and the ability to live any lifestyle that you desire. Whether you want to live cozily in your home or travel the world, you can do anything you want when you put in the effort and grow your business effectively.

It is important that you realize that as great as this book is, there is always more you need to learn. Staying dedicated to learning and focusing on what more you can do to generate success are great ways to continue growing and establishing a stronger business for yourself. The more you devote to learning about what marketing strategies exist and how you can make the most of them, the better chance at success you are going to have.

Marketing is constantly changing, and new strategies are always being added. Taking the time to learn about what these strategies are, how they work, and how you can incorporate them into an attraction marketing method is a great way to continue growing your business. If you want to continue growing, you have to stay relevant.

The next thing you should do after reading this book is start laying a strong foundation for your business. Use the steps that I provided you to find the best company for you to join. Then, go ahead and get started with that company. Once you have, you can begin applying the marketing tools that I taught you so that you can begin getting the word out there. If you can, it would be beneficial for you to find a few blogs or podcasters who are in the MLM industry as well. That way, you can follow them and listen to their podcasts or read their posts to gain more inspiration. Make sure that you follow people who are actually generating great results so that you do not begin picking up on and practicing negative or difficult marketing strategies. Remember: your reputation is important, and a few bad marketing moves can really mess it up.

As you continue growing, always look for opportunities to learn more and do better. Even though you are marketing yourself as the expert, every true expert knows that there is never a cap on how much you can learn. Putting in the effort to constantly learn and grow ensures that you will stay an expert and that people will continue coming to you over anyone else when it comes to the services or products that you offer.

In addition to focusing on your growth in your industry, you also need to focus on your growth as a leader. The more people that are recruited under you, the more you are going to need to step up and lead your team effectively. Take the time to learn how to be an effective leader so that people feel confident being led by you and that they come to you instead of any other potential leaders.

Lastly, if you enjoyed this book, please take the time to honestly rate it on Amazon Kindle. Your feedback would be greatly appreciated.

Thank you, and good luck!

Finally, if you found this book useful in any way, a review on Amazon is always appreciated!